STEALING
GENIUS

STEALING GENIUS

THE SEVEN LEVELS OF
ADAPTIVE INNOVATION

STEVE MILLER

Published and distributed by:
SOUND WISDOM
P.O. Box 310
Shippensburg, PA 17257-0310
717-530-2122

info@soundwisdom.com

www.soundwisdom.com

ISBN 13 TP: 978-1-64095-343-7

ISBN 13 eBook: 978-1-64095-344-4

For Worldwide Distribution, Printed in the U.S.A.

1 2 3 4 5 6 7 8 / 26 25 24 23 22

To all the ladies I love.
You know who you are.

CONTENTS

THE DISTINCTION BETWEEN INNOVATION AND IMPROVEMENT

"Immature poets imitate; mature poets steal."
—T. S. Eliot

To be honest, I was a bit taken aback by the impact that my first book, **Uncopyable: How to Create an Unfair Advantage Over Your Competition**, had when it came out in 2017. The book quickly became a bestseller. *Kirkus Reviews* said it offered a "wealth of actionable information"; business leaders seemed to agree. So many people asked for an expanded version of it that the publisher asked me to put together a second edition…and that expanded edition is, as I write this, still showing up strongly in three different categories: Customer Relations, Strategic Business Planning, and Sales and Selling. After the second version of **Uncopyable** came out, my publisher asked me to write this book based on chapter 4, "Uncopyable Innovation: Stealing Genius™."

Frankly, I'm an innovation geek, so heck yeah.

In his book *The Essential Drucker*, Peter Drucker writes, "Because its purpose is to create a customer, the business enterprise has two—and only these two—basic functions: marketing and innovation."

I agree 100 percent with that statement and, as such, have for 35-plus years focused my consulting, speaking, and publishing on those two areas. Marketing is, very simply, the messaging and communications we send out to our "moose," or target client profile (see Stealing Genius Level 1 below). And because people won't buy from us when we're similar to the competition, innovation is what makes us uniquely, relevantly, and valuably different. I call it being *Uncopyable*.

This book focuses on the innovation side. When I start a conversation about innovation with a new client, I'll often start with something like this: "Hey, when you're tasked with brainstorming, when you need to come up with a new idea, what's the usual process?"

Generally, I hear back: "Well, the usual process is we call the team together, we go into a meeting room, and we have a big flip chart up there, and we say, 'Okay, let's start brainstorming. We want to, you know, separate ourselves from the competition.'"

And I'll ask, "What happens?"

"For a while, everybody just kind of sits there and looks blankly at the flip chart. And then ultimately, somebody says something along the lines of 'Well, hey, you know, our competitor, the ABC Company, they're doing X. We could do that but do it better.' And that's what we do."

I am here to tell you that process actually puts you at a competitive disadvantage.

There is a major misunderstanding in organizations today about what constitutes innovation—about what innovation *is*. Most people I talk to about this give me answers like the one I just shared with you, and they imagine that they are talking about innovation. They're not. They're talking about *improvement*, which is something entirely different.

Improvement is not innovation…and innovation is essential if your aim is to win the battle in today's business environment.

Stealing Genius is a manifesto for leaders who know the difference and are ready, willing, and able to invest their time, attention, and resources into innovation. It is a user's manual for engineering a dramatic, and long-overdue, shift in strategic thinking. The beauty is, once you have learned this process you can apply it anywhere.

Unfortunately, most executives and decision-makers I talk to are focused on *improving* what they already have. I blame the *Continuous Improvement* philosophy for this. They want *better* versions of the products and services they already know about…better versions of what they (or their direct competition) already produce and are familiar with…better variations on processes that are already in place in their organizations. But there's a problem. Fixating on *improvement* in today's world is a dangerous path, a path that ultimately leads to commoditization and irrelevance.

Targeting our time, attention, and resources on *innovation*, by contrast, means identifying something that does not exist right now in any form within our industry or marketplace—something that will create a powerful, emotional, Uncopyable experience for our target customer.

Fixating on improvement and forgetting innovation is a path that ultimately leads to commoditization and irrelevance.

I believe that in order to succeed in today's marketplace, we need the adaptive innovation strategy I call *Stealing Genius*™ to separate ourselves definitively from the competition. How? By delivering a customer experience that the competition either cannot or will not attempt to copy…or even better, that the competition will, as a practical matter, be unable to copy. This is literally impossible if we stick to what is already familiar to us, because whatever is familiar to us and our customers is likely to be familiar to our competition. We must create a new experience that is unique to us and that builds a powerful emotional attachment with our target customer.

In this book, I'll share a proven process developed and honed over 35 years for creating such an experience. The steps that will make Stealing Genius a practical and cultural reality in your world are:

- **FOUNDATIONAL CONCEPT: STEAL GENIUS FROM ALIEN OBSERVATION.** Look well outside what you and your organization are already familiar with. Don't just think outside the box. Build a new box!

- **LEVEL 1: ASK, "WHAT ARE WE TRYING TO FIX?"** Identify the pressing problem or issue that does the best job of pinpointing your "moose"—the distinctive customer/client profile you are hunting for. What "alien," or entity/organization outside our industry or primary realm of experience, do we know that is already very good at addressing that problem or issue? What can we learn from them?

- **LEVEL 2: LOOK TO ORGANIZATIONS OUTSIDE YOUR INDUSTRY THAT YOU ADMIRE.** Move beyond your industry or specialty. Choose an organization that delivers a powerful, Uncopyable experience and see how what they do might apply to the people you serve.

- **LEVEL 3: ASK YOURSELF, "WHAT WOULD MY ROLE MODEL DO?"** Find your personal hero, living or dead, accessible or inaccessible. Put that person or organization in your world. Figure out what kind of experience they would deliver and how they would deliver it. Follow their example.

- **LEVEL 4: FLIP THE COMPETITION.** Do something that is the polar opposite of what people in your industry are currently doing.

- **LEVEL 5: KEEP YOUR RADAR UP 24/7.** This is the consolidation of Phases 1–4: recognizing that sources of Adaptive Innovation[1] can show up anywhere in your own daily experience.

- **LEVEL 6: ORCHESTRATE THE CUSTOMER EXPERIENCE.**
  Create an end-user experience that the competition cannot
  or will not be able to match.

- **LEVEL 7: CONSIDER BRINGING IN A STEALING GENIUS™
  SENSEI.** Shake things up. Bring in someone who specializes
  in helping you create an Uncopyable strategy for identifying, reaching, and emotionally connecting with your target
  customer—your "moose."

Make no mistake. The Stealing Genius™ process is a game-changer.

A TRUE STORY OF STEALING GENIUS

Imagine it's the year 1962. Let's say you have been tasked with the
goal of winning market share with music enthusiasts. How would you
do that?

The "improvement" mindset would tell you to pose this question:
How are most manufacturers winning market share with music enthusiasts and audiophiles? Simple: By building bigger and better record
players. In the 1962 audio market, the focus was almost entirely on
record players: players with bigger speakers, players with higher fidel-
ity to the stereophonic LPs consumers couldn't seem to get enough of,
players that combined their technology with that of radio receivers,
players with handsome wood paneling that looked more and more like
expensive pieces of furniture. Record players were selling like hotcakes.
So it's not all that surprising they were what most people in the field
were thinking about.

A guy my dad, Ralph, ultimately met, however, had a very different
idea. He had the "innovation" mindset.

This friend of my dad's wanted to do the exact opposite of what the record player manufacturers were doing. The thinking he shared with my dad went as follows:

> **Question:** *What's the key negative factor of a record player?*
>
> **Answer:** *It can't move from point A to point B while it plays. It has to stand totally still. The slightest movement makes the needle skip.*

Even portable phonographs, which had been around since at least the 1920s, had to be totally stationary when you operated them. And in the early 1960s, this fellow noticed, consumers were on the move. The interstate highway system revolutionized the way people worked, played, and vacationed. Automobile manufacturers were setting all kinds of new sales records. Playing *audio* records in a moving vehicle, however, remained a distant dream.

Mind you, some people tried—and failed—to give this option to consumers. In 1956, Chrysler introduced Highway Hi-Fi, an expensive optional turntable mounted below an automobile's dashboard that boasted something called "elastic three-point suspension," which made it "almost impossible" (according to Chrysler's ad copy) to jar the needle off the record. The system played special seven-inch discs that rotated at 16 ⅔ rotations per minute, yielding roughly 45 minutes of audio. Highway Hi-Fi had been tested and had apparently functioned well in high-end Chrysler vehicles that offered great suspension and shock absorption. But in an alarming example of short-sighted decision-making, the mounted players were also offered as options in far less expensive vehicles—vehicles that had not been tested at all with the player. These cars, which turned out to be the vast majority of the vehicles Chrysler actually equipped with the expensive optional units, took bumps and potholes far less smoothly than their luxury Chrysler counterparts. The end result was that most of the people who shelled out the money for these players ended up concluding, correctly, that they were incapable of playing Chrysler's (very limited) collection of available recordings without skipping wildly every time the car encountered a pothole or drove across a railroad track. The Highway Hi-Fi option became something of an industry joke, and Chrysler quickly walked away from the whole project. So beyond changing the radio station, millions of drivers had no control over what they listened to while out on the road.

Was that the way it had to be? Maybe not. With so many people on the move, my dad's future partner wondered, what powerful new experience could you give people if you somehow found a way to do what Chrysler had tried and failed to do—put the power to play the music of the consumer's choice inside their car?

The man's name was Bill Lear, and I'll bet you've heard of his corporate aircraft. Yes—we're talking about that Bill Lear, the founder of the Lear Jet Corporation.

Lear's idea was revolutionary. What I want you to notice, though, is it was the exact opposite of what most people in the marketplace were doing at the time. But his idea was, as it turned out, the key to the next great leap forward in consumer audio. And it was all about innovation—not improvement. It was something utterly new to the consumer.

Lear asked my dad—an audio specialist—to work on the idea with him, and pretty soon they had come up with a prototype of what they called the Lear Jet Stereo 8 cartridge, as well as a prototype of the player that turned what had been recorded on that cartridge into high-quality portable audio. Today, we are more likely to call what they came up with an 8-track tape player; that's what Lear, my dad, and a few other people invented.

I still remember Dad and his team working 24/7 for weeks to develop a prototype for the Summer Consumer Electronics Show in Chicago. He even bought a seat on the plane for this industry-changing product.

They pitched the prototype—and the experience of portable consumer-driven music choices—to auto executives. They loved it. Working with the auto industry, Lear and his allies wove the new technology into the American psyche. By the late 1960s, the 8-track segment dominated the consumer audio market, and the explosive popularity of 8-track systems in cars had ignited heavy demand for home and portable units—all because Lear was willing to think about a consumer experience based on the idea that he could build something that did something record players were incapable of doing.

But I'm getting ahead of myself. To manufacture the cassettes and players they had invented, Lear and the other members of his team originally set up manufacturing facilities in Detroit, Michigan, then Nogales, Mexico. Both places had unique problems. My father had experience working in Japan and suggested they take a look at setting up production over there.

However, Lear wanted to make sure the products coming out of the factory were the highest possible quality. Back in the 1960s, "Made in Japan" products were inferior, so they went looking for help. My dad heard of an American consultant—someone whose ideas didn't catch on with big American manufacturers but who had worked for Toyota in Japan. His name was W. Edwards Deming. Deming was the creator of what is known as Total Quality Management or TQM. TQM can be summarized as a management system for a customer-focused organization that involves all employees in continual improvement.

Lear interviewed and hired him. This was, of course, long before Deming had become legendary in quality circles for his work as an engineer, statistician, professor, author, lecturer, and management consultant.

There they were, my dad, Mr. Lear, and Mr. Deming. As a wiseass teenager, I called them the Three Stooges under my breath. Of course, they were far from that.

On the road a lot, Dad thought he needed to spend quality time with his teenage son and, bewilderingly, figured I might even benefit from hanging out with the three of them. So he dragged me along on some of their trips. Full disclosure: audio component manufacturing was the last thing in the world I would have chosen to focus on—after all, I was only 13 years old. My main memory of those meetings is being bored half to death as the three men talked. Yet something stuck deep in my tiny little male teenager brain—something that remained latent, waiting to resurface when a chance conversation came, years later, that would enable it to be put to proper use.

Let me be very clear: I had no interest whatsoever in hanging out with these guys. I was not a participant. I was an unhappy teenage observer who had much more important things he would have rather been doing—playing baseball, golf, or basketball, for instance. I did not want to be there. I didn't realize it at the time, of course, but I was witnessing history. This is one of the reasons friends sometimes call me "Forrest Gump": I have this unexplainable and serendipitous ability to wander into important events—and eventually connect the dots and learn from those events! This was certainly one of those times.

Years later, when the moment was exactly right, something would trigger that memory, a very important connection to something said on those boring, interminable occasions. As I realized the powerful lessons I'd been exposed to at a young age, I became a modest but devoted student of both Lear and Deming, researching their philosophies and recollecting conversations to which I had been privy. Both men heavily impacted my view of business, competition, and innovation.

Below are highlights from what I heard Mr. Deming say during those discussions with Lear and my dad:

- *Total quality.* I clearly remember Deming emphasizing the operative word being *total*, which is a way of looking at running an organization that is very different from what most executives are used to. It's a way of running your entire organization—maybe even running your entire life—based on assumptions that most companies, and in particular most American companies (as Deming often pointed out), are not willing to take on, because they're not comfortable with those assumptions. This is as true today, I am afraid, as it was in 1962.

- One of those assumptions is that *benchmarking is a critical tool.* It needs to happen everywhere in the organization. Again, the operative word in the phrase *total quality* is *total.* People can get distracted by the word *quality* and forget it is meant to apply to every aspect of the organization.

- What is benchmarking? Basically, it means you *observe correct behavior and then emulate it within your own context.*

- There are two kinds of benchmarking. This is huge. The first kind is *intrinsic benchmarking*. With intrinsic benchmarking, you study the world with which you are already familiar. You study your own organization. You study your competitors. You study what's happening in your own industry. And you implement, monitor, and, if possible, improve on the best practices you've studied. This is the "box" we hear so much about.

  Intrinsic benchmarking is primarily figuring out where you stand in comparison to the competition. The idea is to at least match what is already expected by the customer, based on what they have experienced from your competitors. At a very minimum, you have to match what the competition offers, because you certainly do not want to fall below that standard. Essentially, it's the ante to be in the game, but you will not get any innovative, competitive strategies or tactics from intrinsic benchmarking.

- The second kind of benchmarking (which I can recall Deming saying the vast majority of American companies did *not* embrace) is *extrinsic benchmarking*. This is where you seek out people, organizations, and teams (I call them "aliens") that have *nothing at all* to do with what your own organization, your own industry, and your own market are doing… and you identify, implement, and monitor best practices from those places, too. Studying other "alien" boxes can reveal practices that might be common in another industry yet groundbreaking in yours! That's the essence of Stealing Genius.

There are two types of benchmarking, both of which are essential: intrinsic and extrinsic.

These are, in broad outline, the principles Deming used to make Toyota (and, beyond Toyota, large segments of the entire postwar

Japanese economy) globally competitive in a way they had never before been.[2]

These discussions between my dad, Lear, and Deming were the first of several serendipitous accidents in my life that ended up pointing me toward what would eventually become my calling: innovation. I wonder how different my world would be if my dad had not dragged me along to those meetings. In hindsight, I guess it's good he did. Now I can share with you the ideas about innovation that Deming shared with Lear, my dad, and (indirectly) me—ideas that, for some reason I cannot quite fathom, stuck with me when I was a 13-year-old and ended up changing my life, and the businesses of my clients, dramatically for the better.

At the time, however, I did what a lot of Americans do when first exposed to these ideas: I ignored them. I thought they were irrelevant to my world and my experience. Heck, I was only 13.

And then came the day in the late 1980s when I met Jim Nordstrom.

Nordstrom, at that time, was the co-president of the legendary chain of Nordstrom specialty fashion stores. The company was (and is) virtually synonymous with world-class customer service, and Nordstrom himself was the prime mover and shaker who created, lived, and evangelized the values that produced that reputation. If for some reason you think you haven't heard of Nordstrom's legendary reputation for putting the customer first and honoring its famous unconditional-guarantee policy, I'm going to bet you're wrong. Why? Because I have yet to run into someone who hasn't heard some form of the story below at least once. It appeared in a 1989 *Newsweek* article referencing a Fairbanks, Alaska, Nordstrom outlet...but it has been told and retold in countless media and on countless platforms since then.

The customer wanted to return a tire. Never mind that the Nordstrom department-store chain sells upscale clothing, not automotive parts. According to company lore, the clerk accepted the tire (and refunded the money) because that's what the customer wanted.

This may be the single most influential customer service story of modern times. It's certainly among the most widely circulated. When a mutual acquaintance introduced me to Nordstrom and suggested I book a meeting with him to discuss a sports sponsorship project I was working on, I followed up and set the meeting. As the day rolled around, I made my way into the co-president's (surprisingly modest) office. I had two items on my agenda: to determine whether Nordstrom would consider sponsoring a new golf tournament I was working on and whether the story about the clerk giving the customer a full refund on tires that he had bought somewhere else was true. Of course, I asked about the tire story first.

Jim Nordstrom smiled at me enigmatically and said, "I wouldn't know. I wasn't there." That's as good an example of an answer that's actually a non-answer from a senior corporate leader as I've ever come across.[3]

Nordstrom was a personable man, although a little quieter than I expected. He was easy enough to talk to, which is not always the case when you are dealing with someone in his position. I enjoyed our conversation, and I got the feeling he did, too. He was unpretentious and as sharp as a tack. This was quite a while back, so I don't remember everything he and I talked about, but I do remember it turned out he was interested in continuing the discussion about sponsoring the golf event I had come there to talk about. Eventually, however, the fates intervened, and the event I was planning fell through (I won't bore you with the details about why). Before that, however, he and I had a couple meetings, and we shared our philosophies and ideas on marketing and promotion.

During one of those meetings, I was astonished to hear the legendary co-president of Nordstrom say to me, "Steve, I've been talking to a couple of people here, and we've been thinking it would be a good idea to have you do some work for us."

Not only was this not what I had expected from our conversation—it wasn't even in the realm of what I had considered remotely possible.

I said, "That's certainly flattering, but I don't really think it would work out. I do a lot of consulting, but I have absolutely zero retail experience. In fact, I have zero business-to-consumer experience! I'm a business-to-business guy. I really don't think I'm who you want. I have no idea how to sell soft goods." I wasn't negotiating. I wasn't playing games. I didn't want to make a fool of myself. I knew absolutely nothing about Nordstrom's business and didn't want to pretend I did!

Without missing a beat, Nordstrom said to me, "Yeah—I know. That's exactly why we want to hire you."

I said, "What do you mean?"

He said, "Well, if we go out and hire a retail consultant, what is that consultant going to do? They're just going to tell us the same thing he or she might tell our competitors, right? We want you to come on board so you can tell us things from outside of our industry. You tell us what you've seen and what's working elsewhere. And when you do, you'll be telling us things we would not be able to hear from anyone else. You might give us some new ideas. That's why I want you to come work for us."

Surprised, I had to admit to myself that at the very least, the man knew what he wanted. And who was I to second-guess his analysis? I shook his hand and agreed to do some work for Nordstrom.[4]

Driving home from that meeting, I had an epiphany: *What Nordstrom had been talking about was exactly what Deming had been talking about with my dad and Lear, two and a half decades earlier!*

It was like a little light bulb switched on in my head. What Nordstrom asked me to provide his chain of stores with was what Deming had called *extrinsic benchmarking.* Nordstrom didn't *just* want to study what people in his industry were doing to keep customers happy. He did want to know about that, of course, so he could meet and exceed customer expectations. But he knew that wasn't enough. He wanted to know what people *outside* of his industry were doing so he could adapt best practices from them, as well.

That epiphany, following that meeting with Jim Nordstrom, marked the beginning of the innovation technique I now call Stealing Genius.

REDEFINING INNOVATION

Most of the people I work with now begin our relationship exactly where I was at the beginning of my fateful conversation with Nordstrom. They are used to looking at innovation in a way that is quite different from the way people like Deming and Nordstrom look at it and the way I now look at it. I now know that confusing innovation with improvement is an invitation for a dangerous and deepening irrelevance in the marketplace.

My mission—and this book—are about helping leaders and their teams get a clearer sense of *true* innovation…the kind of innovation that makes them literally Uncopyable in the marketplace!

And just so we're clear, that was what my epiphany was all about. That moment of clarity as I drove back from my discussion with Nordstrom was my first glimpse of the kind of innovation Deming had in mind—the kind of innovation that Nordstrom was ready, willing, and eager to pay for.[5]

That's what we'll be looking at together. That's the transition I'll be helping you make. And it *is*, inevitably, a transition. We start out thinking about intrinsic benchmarking…thinking (as indeed the vast majority of leaders still think) that is the only kind of benchmarking that exists. It's natural enough to want to begin the discussion by looking at that with which you are already familiar. It's natural enough to think, *Okay, time to innovate. I wonder how the competition is innovating. Hmm…let's do a Google search on them. Well, it says in this press release their machine is making 5,000 widgets a month. You know what we're going to do? We're going to find a way to build a machine that makes 7,000 widgets a month, and then we'll have innovated the heck out of them and we'll have an advantage in the marketplace.*

Maybe it's better, and yes, you might have an advantage for a brief time, but it's not innovation.

Say you do start making 7,000 widgets a month—do you know what's going to happen? Of course you do. That competitor, or another one, is going to watch you and see what you're up to, and then they're going to say, "I see where they've got a machine that makes 7,000 widgets a month. But you know what? We can find a way to build one that makes 10,000 widgets a month." And on and on the cycle goes. This is the path to commoditization. Pretty soon everyone in your industry is offering essentially what you offer. Competition does not breed innovation. It breeds conformity.

Competition does not breed innovation. It breeds conformity.

Relying on intrinsic benchmarking for all of your ideas is a lot like being in an echo chamber. Lots of sound. Lots of reverberation. Not a lot of meaningful information.

Any sustainable competitive advantage in the marketplace you may think you derive from a process like what I've just described is basically a mirage. You think the advantage is real. But it's ethereal and brief. You think you can reach out and touch it. And for a moment it seems as though you can, but then it slips away into nothingness.

In order to get *truly* new ideas that make you and your organization Uncopyable, you have to study people, teams, organizations, and experiences that have nothing to do with your world—what I call your "box." This is what people mean when they tell us to "think outside the box." You have to get out of that box. But what the heck does that really mean? You climb out and then what?

I'll tell you what is better than thinking outside the box: *building your own box.* You build a brand-new box and fill it with truly innovative customer experiences…unique, never-before-seen products or services…new processes…new language…new rules of competition… and true attachment, not just loyalty, with your clients. You build a box that becomes very difficult, if not impossible, for competitors to copy and improve upon. You become UNCOPYABLE.

Don't think outside the box. Build your own box.

In order to do that, you have to go out and study what I like to call "alien sources." There are a number of effective ways to do this. But the core concept of searching out these influences is important enough for us to spend some time looking at it in depth. That's what we will start doing in the next chapter.

THE BIG TAKEAWAY:

Improvement is not innovation. Build your own box.

DO THIS:

Outline the usual process you use when tasked with brainstorming a new idea.

- How much of the process involves studying the competition for ideas?
- How much of this process involves *improvement*?
- How much involves *innovation*?
- Understand, and be ready to explain to others on your team, both essential types of benchmarking: intrinsic and extrinsic.

To truly get "outside the box," you have to build a new box. Throw out your old strategies that operate based on comparison—trying to "one-up" your competition—and get ready to identify and consult completely new sources of inspiration.

GET THE "STEALING GENIUS FIELD GUIDE" PLUS MORE USEFUL INFORMATION AND TIPS! GO TO:

stealinggenius.com/resources

NOTES

1. Adaptive innovation is all about the discovery process itself, where there is no specific goal of innovation. The story of George de Mestral's walk in the forest, which you'll encounter in the next chapter, is a perfect example. He wasn't specifically looking for a replacement for the zipper, but by being open to possibilities, he did. New ideas can come from anywhere.

2. Deming's enduring impact on Japan can be glimpsed in the fact that the annual Deming Prize, perhaps the highest honor in the world for achievements in Total Quality Management (TQM), was named after him. The prize, sponsored by the Japanese Union of Scientists and Engineers, originated in Japan in 1951.

3. For the record, the urban-myth-busting site Snopes.com has investigated the matter and has concluded there are enough competing, and implausible, versions of the tire-refund story circulating to support a verdict of "apocryphal." It still bugs me when I hear a professional speaker or read a business book claiming it is true.

   The underlying principle the story supports, however—that Nordstrom gives "no-questions-asked" refunds when other stores won't, and that it stands behind its unconditional-refund policy in the most seemingly unlikely of circumstances—is something my family can attest to personally. Our daughter Kelly visited Nordstrom a while back and was trying on some shoes. The clerk helping her asked, "Do you have any other shoes from Nordstrom?"

Kelly said, "Yes, I have a pair of shoes from your store. I don't wear them a lot, though."

The clerk asked, "Why is that?"

"Well," Kelly explained, "every time I put them on, they pinch my feet, so I don't wear them very often. They look great, and I do wear them occasionally, but I don't make a habit of wearing them because they're a little painful. I think I bought them a half-size too small."

The clerk instantly said, "Oh, bring them back. We'll give you a refund." Kelly, who didn't want to take advantage of the store or get the clerk in trouble, said, "Oh, no. I couldn't. I've had those shoes for maybe three years, and I still do wear them sometimes. I just mentioned them because you asked." The clerk looked her straight in the eye and said, "Please bring them back for a refund. Every time you put those shoes on, you think of Nordstrom!" Kelly brought the shoes back.

4. This was not the first time my unusual career background, which encompasses not only pro golf but also stints in the copper mines of Arizona and work in Hollywood movies and TV, led to my taking on the role of the "outside alien who might bring an interesting perspective to the conversation." Nor would it be the last. You could say I've turned being an outsider into a professional calling.

5. I am sometimes asked to talk about the work I did for Nordstrom. I suspect the biggest impact I had there came about in early discussions regarding the importance of sharing memorable narratives of positive customer experiences, narratives people would be likely to share with friends and family. These stories comprise what I call the Nordstrom Myth.

Ideas for Stealing Genius

THE FOUNDATIONAL CONCEPT: STEAL GENIUS FROM ALIENS

"Genius means little more than the faculty of perceiving in an unhabitual way."

—William James

There is an urban legend, widely circulated, that NASA "invented" Velcro during the Space Race years of the early and mid-1960s. The truth is more interesting—and more illuminating.

That word *invention* isn't my favorite, since it seems to imply that a good idea materialized more or less out of nowhere. That's just not so. Innovations rarely spring up out of nowhere. They usually have a source. Once we identify that source, we can get deeper clarity on the process by which *we* can create new breakthroughs of our own.

Here's what *is* true: When NASA found itself in need of a reliable replacement for the zipper, which was not ideal for use by astronauts in a zero-gravity environment, its team leaders started looking around for alternatives. They didn't need a better zipper; they needed a totally new and innovative solution. They found a company in Switzerland that offered such an alternative and opted to give that company a contract in the early 1960s. *That* was the point at which the US space program started using the (now-ubiquitous) hook-and-loop touch fastening system known as Velcro on all kinds of things: spacesuits, pockets on other kinds of clothing, helmets, food and drink ports, and stuff like pens and packets they didn't want to see floating around the space capsule. Each design was highly customized by NASA engineers to the specific application the astronauts would be using. But NASA did not invent this technology.

Innovations rarely spring up out of nowhere. They usually have an alien source.

The company NASA reached out to is still in operation today. It's Velcro SA, a firm founded by a Swiss electrical engineer by the name of George de Mestral. It was de Mestral who invented Velcro back in the 1940s. And the means by which he did this is a classic example of Stealing Genius.

Back in 1941, de Mestral went on a walk along the mountain paths of the Swiss Alps with his dog Milka. He wasn't thinking about fastening systems or spaceships or moon landings. He was thinking, first and foremost, about *relaxation*…but he was, crucially, keeping his mind open to new ideas and unexpected phenomena, which is one of the major requirements of Stealing Genius Level 5 ("Keep Your Radar Up 24/7"). The Zen Buddhists have a saying: *In the beginner's mind there are many possibilities; in the expert's mind there are few.* As he completed his walk with Milka, de Mestral was, we might say, firmly connected to his beginner's mind.

It was that beginner's mind that allowed him to take an experience others might have simply considered an inconvenience—the burrs he had to extract from Milka's coat and also from his own woolen socks and coat—and ask a simple, powerful question: *What is really happening here?*

De Mestral concluded that what was really happening was millions of years of evolution had given the burdock plant—the source of those burrs he had to brush out of his dog's coat—a powerful bonding strategy. This strategy enabled burdock to propagate its species by spreading its seeds far and wide, throughout the Alps and beyond. At this point, de Mestral asked himself another simple, powerful question: *Where else could this be used?*

The answer, he concluded, was just about anywhere people needed to fasten something to something else. De Mestral was what I call a Stealing Genius Black Belt. I'll talk more about the technique he used in chapter 6.

By studying something *already happening in nature*, de Mestral came up with a new application. Velcro, of course, is a fastening system made up of two components: a fabric strip featuring hundreds of tiny hooks (analogous to the burdock seeds) capable of "mating" with another fabric strip featuring hundreds of tiny loops (analogous to Milka's coat and de Mestral's woolen socks and coat). The result: two elements that would attach strongly *but temporarily*, disengaging when pulled apart. His original prototype featured strips made of cotton, a material that presented a number of logistical problems; eventually de Mestral settled on a system that used nylon and polyester. He called the new system Velcro, which was a combination of the French words *velour* (velvet) and *crochet* (hook). (Sidenote: The word *Velcro* is both a registered trademark for the fastening system, which de Mestral was wise enough to patent, and the name of the company that produces it.)

So there you have it. Because NASA was looking for a totally innovative solution to their zipper problem, they discovered Velcro. And because George de Mestral was open to an *alien source* of ideas, he was able to develop Velcro…a system that helped human beings go to the moon! That's Stealing Genius in a nutshell.

Those two questions are worth remembering:

What is really happening here?

Where else could this be used?

THE BIG IDEA

The big idea behind Stealing Genius is simply that, like de Mestral, we want to be *open to the possibility of breakthroughs coming from areas that are well beyond our industry, our company, or our normal areas of focus when we are at work.*

This means accepting a certain amount of not-knowing as part of the process, which can be a little uncomfortable for some people at first. When we make a conscious decision to move outside of our own areas of expertise, we will not know exactly what the breakthroughs are going to be; or how, in a narrow sense, they are likely to connect to our organizational strategy; or what specific steps we are going to need to take to adapt them to the world of the customers we aim to serve. But we need to be open to those breakthroughs nonetheless. And that takes practice, because most of us are used to thinking of the burrs we find in our socks and dog's coat after a walk through the wilderness as petty inconveniences…when in fact they may be so much more. They may be the key to an Uncopyable Advantage.

One of the most fascinating and inspiring areas of innovation rooted in the driving principle of Stealing Genius is the one de Mestral followed to huge commercial and practical success: *biomimicry*, which has been defined as "the design and production of materials, structures, and systems that are modeled on biological entities and processes." In this chapter, we're going to take a close look at some of the more astonishing examples of this powerful strategy on record. I'm spending some time on this example of Stealing Genius for two reasons: first, because biomimicry perfectly captures and exemplifies, in an easy-to-understand way, the big idea of this book, and second, because it's a path to innovation that is open to virtually everyone.

De Mestral is perhaps the most famous and commercially successful example of a practical implementation of biomimicry. But there are plenty of others. Let's look at them, and at the field as a whole, right now.

BIOMIMICRY AND
THE NEGLECTED ART OF DESPECIALIZATION

The path to innovation we are discussing goes by several different names in the scientific community. Some researchers have called it *biomimicry*; others have called it *biomimetics* or *biophysics* or *bionics*. (The term *bionics* has fallen out of favor in recent years, thanks to the confusion stirred up by the 1970s television series *The Six Million Dollar Man* and *The Bionic Woman*.) My favorite quote from a scientist on the underlying meaning and direction of these various terms comes from the American researcher Otto Herbert Schmitt, who wrote:

> Biophysics is not so much a subject matter as it is a point of view. It is an approach to problems of biological science utilizing the theory and technology of the physical sciences. Conversely, biophysics is also a biologist's approach to problems of physical science and engineering, although this aspect has largely been neglected.

This is Stealing Genius, translated into terms a scientist might use. The disciplines of biological science and physical science are very different, yet Schmitt was arguing for a "point of view" that resulted from an expert in one field taking on the perspective of someone with deep experience in the other field. Schmitt's meaning becomes even clearer when you look at a speech he made some years later, in which he said:

> Let us consider what bionics has come to mean operationally and what it or some word like it (I prefer biomimetics) ought to mean in order to make good use of the technical skills of scientists specializing, or rather, I should say, despecializing into this area of research.

That word *despecializing* is the one to which I want to draw your attention. Stealing Genius demands despecialization. It demands a willingness to step away from the industry, the discipline, the surroundings, the questions you are most familiar with…so you can look at other industries, other academic disciplines, other surroundings, other questions that lead you, eventually, to the two questions we posed earlier:

What is really happening here?

Where else could this be used?

Despecialization is an art— a neglected one.

Despecialization is an art—a neglected one. It takes a conscious choice to despecialize—to set aside your own status as an expert—in order to generate meaningful breakthroughs. Let's look now at some specific examples of what the willingness to despecialize has made possible when people with deep experience in a certain field chose to set aside their own expertise for a moment...so they could open themselves up to the possibility of becoming inspired by the models, systems, and elements of nature to solve complex human problems.

A FEW MORE EXAMPLES OF STEALING GENIUS FROM ALIENS

Here are some of the more notable examples that have produced advances in engineering, manufacturing, and consumer products. Each is, by definition, an example of utilizing an alien experience for inspiration.

- One of the oldest examples is Johannes Gutenberg's printing press. He based this world-changing invention on the screw press, first created and used by the Romans in the first century AD for wine and olive oil production.

- The streamlined design of the Japanese Shinkansen 500 series high-speed train was inspired by the aerodynamically optimal beak of the kingfisher bird.

- 3M developed a breakthrough concept for preventing infections associated with surgery after getting input from a theatrical makeup specialist who was knowledgeable about preventing facial skin infections.

- Naval engineer Richard James was developing sensitive springs meant to keep fragile equipment steady on ships. James knocked one of his new springs from a shelf and watched it make the now-famous Slinky walk down the stairs instead of just hitting the ground. *Time* magazine named Slinky one of the greatest toys of all time.

- After Alfred Southwick heard the story of a drunken dock worker named George Lemuel Smith dying instantly from touching an electric generator, he conceived the idea of electrical execution. Southwick was a dentist and used one of his dental chairs as the method, thus inventing the "electric chair."

- Urban one-way road systems were directly inspired by the blood circulation system in the human body. Of course, they were! Cities are alive!

THE BIG TAKEAWAY:

Search out an alien source that can drive innovation. Start by despecializing: take off your expert hat.

DO THIS:

Consider three processes that occur in nature or in the material world. They can, and likely should, be totally unrelated to your question or challenge. Analyze each process, and determine whether it could serve as a source of alien inspiration, by asking:

- What is really happening here?
- Where else could this be used?

Consider keeping a journal to record the answers to these questions.

GET THE "STEALING GENIUS FIELD GUIDE" PLUS MORE USEFUL INFORMATION AND TIPS! GO TO:

stealinggenius.com/resources

Ideas for Stealing Genius

CH 2

STEALING GENIUS LEVEL 1: ASK, "WHAT ARE WE TRYING TO FIX?"

> ## "If your only tool is a hammer, then every problem looks like a nail."
>
> ## —Abraham Maslow

The first level of Stealing Genius is to start by identifying exactly what problem you are trying to solve.

Innovation usually does not unfold in a vacuum. Most of the time, it requires a purpose, an objective, a committed focus. You have to be willing to ask yourself, "Who, specifically, are we hoping to serve with this innovation—and what is the specific nature of the challenge we are facing?" If you aren't willing to be both rigorous and consistent in posing and answering those questions, then you won't find the other techniques I will be sharing with you in this book to be of much help. George Harrison has a song with a memorable lyric: "If you don't know where you're going, any road will take you there." That line is worth bearing in mind as you get started.

Only when you know the dimensions of the issue you are trying to fix can you start looking for *aliens* you can study and emulate—people, teams, companies, and organizations that are already very good at solving that particular issue but *don't* operate within your industry, your company, your team, or your immediate circle of professional and personal contacts. Once you identify the problem you are all committed to solving, you can start evaluating alien influences in search of best practices that address that challenge—but not before. That's what Jim Nordstrom was doing. He identified the challenges—customer experience, marketing, repeat business—and then set about identifying and studying alien organizations that were already excellent at doing those things.

IDENTIFYING THE PROBLEM, BUILDING A COALITION

The problem you are aiming to solve could be an internal process that isn't accomplishing what you want it to accomplish. It could be a communication problem within your organization. It could be a strategy you need to revise. It could be an engagement plan for reaching a market you have not yet penetrated that isn't yet delivering the results you were hoping to see. It could be a service issue affecting end users—something that is keeping you from connecting emotionally with your customers, or preventing them from being totally satisfied with your product or service, or failing to inspire them to choose to work with you again after they've worked with you the first time. The problem you face could be a poorly defined purpose or mission for your team or organization. It could be something that touches on all of the above issues. It could be something that touches on none of the above. But whatever it is, it is a *pressing business problem* people are willing and able to devote the time, attention, and financial and human resources necessary to solving.

This question of commitment in terms of money, time, and attention is critically important. The last thing you want to be is very, very good at something nobody wants to pay for. This is why you need to identify not just the problem, but also the stakeholders who have an interest in making sure this problem gets solved. That, too, is an essential part of this first technique. Identifying the problem you are trying to fix means pinpointing, and creating plans with, the people who have a shared interest in making sure the problem gets fixed.

Usually, identifying the problem properly means creating what I call a "What Are We Trying to Fix" Narrative. This is a way of ensuring innovation is an actual priority for the team and the organization—not just something it would be nice to do at some point in the future—by tying the innovation campaign *directly* to a pressing organizational problem.

If there is no working INNOVATION COALITION capable of securing the financial, human, and logistical resources necessary to innovate, build one!

SOLVE FOR X, Y, AND Z:
THE "WHAT ARE WE TRYING TO FIX" NARRATIVE

Here is the formula I use to develop a "What Are We Trying to Fix" narrative. It is relevant if you are an outsider trying to build an Innovation Coalition within an organization you haven't worked with before; it is just as relevant if you are an insider trying to build a coalition.

- *Once someone concludes (VALUE WE DELIVER [X]) is the secret to solving (HIGH-PRIORITY PROBLEM [Y])…*

- *…and also decides the only way to take effective action on what they have concluded is to (CALL TO ACTION [Z])…*

- *…every other issue becomes secondary, we both KNOW WHAT WE ARE TRYING TO FIX, and we secure the time, attention, and financial and human resources necessary to innovate and solve the problem.*

I'll give you a real-life example of what I am talking about. I was working with senior leadership at a company called Charnecke Tents—they're located in Rosholt, Wisconsin. This is a family-owned business that has been around since 1929. They manufacture tents for major events like weddings and receptions. Their problem was they're in a very competitive field. Lots of companies manufacture and rent tents with not a lot of differentiation. After a fair amount of discussion, we concluded that the pressing, high-priority problem Charnecke faced was they were failing to stand out uniquely and relevantly in a crowded market space…and they had an ever-expanding list of competitors focused on delivering cheaper prices. We looked to create a branding proposition that established them not as commodity providers, but as the trusted brand where price wasn't the deciding factor. What story could we tell?

Once we aligned on the problem we both knew needed fixing (the call to action), and once we were certain the resources we needed were there to begin the task of solving the problem, we could start looking for the right aliens to study. Who else had faced this problem of needing to stand out in a crowded, highly competitive market—and how had they done it?

FINDING THE ALIEN SOURCE

We looked at a lot of different possibilities, but one of the most intriguing alien sources we listed was Federal Express. The vast, crowded market they were hoping to stand out in was known broadly, back in the day, as "courier services."

Let me give you some background on this remarkable story. The founder of Federal Express (which eventually rechristened itself as FedEx) was a college student by the name of Frederick W. Smith, who wrote a term paper while he was a student at Yale back in 1965. His paper laid the groundwork for a whole new kind of company, an organization devoted to a concept that would eventually revolutionize the crowded, many-layered shipping and courier delivery market.

What Smith had in mind was a nationwide system that was specifically designed for *urgent* deliveries. His paper proposed that a company carrying small, essential items by plane, from the initial point of pickup to its final destination, could be significantly more efficient than services that relied primarily on surface routes and/or played "tag" with other delivery services to complete the shipment. It was a brilliant idea, one that relied on a "hub-and-spoke" distribution concept Smith had presumably adapted from Delta Airlines, the first US commercial air carrier to put it into practice. The professor was unimpressed. He gave the paper a C.

Fast-forward six years. In 1971, after having graduated from Yale and served a tour of duty in Vietnam, Smith returned to the States and launched his iconoclastic startup company—along with a revolution in the way people look at couriers and shipping as a whole.

Smith's revolution succeeded, of course. Federal Express's "When it absolutely, positively has to be there overnight" strategy definitely did find a way to stand out, as evidenced by the fact that it is today a $17 billion enterprise. The question my client and I were focused on was: *How* did the company create its early foothold in what was known, back in the 1970s and early 1980s, as the "courier services" market?

Here's a hint: If you've read this far, you've just directly experienced FedEx's strategy for standing out. I shared it with you by telling you the story about Smith's low grade on that term paper.

A big part of how the company has achieved and retained what's known as "top-of-mind awareness" with consumers has to do with the FedEx *origin narrative*, the story it tells prospective customers and others (including members of the media) about how the company began. Lots of companies have origin narratives; I can't think of many that have had the impact of FedEx's. This particular origin narrative is a carefully structured, memorable, and true story that has become not only an important element of FedEx's culture, but also part of American business history. It brilliantly leverages Smith's professor's skepticism with his idea, turning the term-paper incident into a quintessential "underdog wins in the end" tale. Here's one classic version of the narrative, from the FedEx website:

In 1965, Yale University undergraduate Frederick W. Smith wrote a term paper that invented an industry and changed what's possible. In the paper, he laid out the logistical challenges facing pioneering firms in the information technology industry. Most airfreight shippers relied on passenger route systems, but those didn't make economic sense for urgent shipments, Smith wrote. He proposed a system specifically designed to accommodate time-sensitive shipments such as medicine, computer parts, and electronics. Smith's professor apparently didn't see the revolutionary implications of his thesis, and the paper received just an average grade.

In August 1971, following a stint in the military, Smith bought controlling interest in Arkansas Aviation Sales, located in Little Rock, Arkansas. While operating his new firm, he saw firsthand how difficult it was to get packages and other airfreight delivered within one to two days. With his term paper in mind, Smith set out to find a better way. Thus the idea for Federal Express was born: A company that has revolutionized global business practices and that now defines speed and reliability.

Take a close look at that brief origin narrative, and consider how many important things it accomplishes in less than 200 words.

- It shares a classic storytelling archetype, the *hero's journey*—in this case, the young hero who triumphs despite the skepticism/opposition of an older authority figure. (Think of Luke Skywalker telling his uncle, early on in the first *Star Wars* film, that he wants to join the Rebellion against the

Empire.) People connect instantly with classic archetypes like that.

- In using that archetype, it gives us a memorable incident that explains why, when, and how FedEx was founded—one that is fun to share with other people. Who says professors at Yale always know best? What's that old saying, *Those who can't do, teach*?

- It tells us exactly what FedEx does best.

- It sets up two concepts that are integral elements of FedEx's brand promise: *speed* and *reliability.*

I knew my client Charnecke Tents had a great origin story, and I was convinced they could achieve a similar effect to the one FedEx had had with *its* origin narrative. We talked about their origin narrative for a long time and began to ask ourselves whether it might be able to accomplish the same things. I knew that, in addition to deploying an archetype, building on a memorable incident, conveying what Charnecke did best, and supporting a brand promise, whatever we came up with together had to generate a YES response to two very important questions:

1. Did it achieve the objective to stand out in a crowded market?

2. Was it moose bait? Meaning, did it target and appeal to a specific group of prospective customers—in this case, rental centers in the Midwest whose clients were planning an important event, such as a wedding reception or a graduation party, scheduled to take place outside?

By the way, I'm guessing that unless you've read my book *Uncopyable*, you weren't expecting the phrase "moose bait." Let me explain.

Very often, when I begin talking with senior leadership about who their target market is, I'll hear something like this in response: "Everybody needs us, because every company can benefit from what our product/service does."

Uh, wrong answer.

Think of yourself (and, by extension, your entire organization) as a hunter. The best hunters are quite particular about what they go out to hunt. A good hunter—one with experience, one who manages to keep the family fed—very quickly learns to focus on a specific type of game. And so should we. We're not going out into the woods to hunt every animal in the forest. We're not going out to hunt whatever we happen to come across. We're going out to hunt a certain animal. We need to know what we are hunting for: moose. Not grouse. Not deer. Not pheasant. Not rabbit. Not wolverines. We're hunting moose. Just moose. That's what we want to bring home. We also need to make sure we know all the relevant habits and activity patterns that connect to moose herds. We need to make sure we're hunting in the right place for moose. And of course we want to bring along the right moose bait.

What's true for hunters is true for us, as well. We need to know exactly whom we're targeting, how they behave, and what they are attracted to. So one big question for the people I work with is this one: *Who is your moose?* Another is: *What kind of moose bait are you using?*

After spending a fair amount of time with the company's senior leadership on all of this, I unearthed a detail that pointed me toward a narrative that might be able to answer both of those questions in the affirmative. While we were still pondering all the paths open to us, I asked my contact, Jenny, how and when the company had come into being. She told me a family story I could tell had been shared many, many times before. Back in 1929, her Grandpa Eddie, eager to supplement an income battered by the Great Depression, had scraped together enough cash to buy a circus tent on the theory he could rent it out and earn some money that way. Sure enough, an opportunity presented itself in the form of a wedding party in search of a tent. Grandpa Eddie arranged the rental and then realized his customer would be needing tables and chairs, too. He arranged for those. And oh, yes, some music. He had his own band for that. And oh, yes, they'll probably need food. Grandpa Eddie arranged for that. And come to think of it, the folks at the wedding would want something to drink as well. At which point Jenny shared the story's well-worn punch line: "Fortunately, he had a still for that part. Yep. Grandpa was a bootlegger."

The instant I heard that punch line, I knew we had struck gold. I said to Jenny: "That's it. That's how you can set yourself apart. With your origin story."

She and others in the leadership were initially skeptical about this idea. After all, they had shared this story only among family and close friends…and wasn't bootlegging *illegal* back in 1929? The answer, of course, was yes…and that, I explained, was what would make the story so memorable. Everyone would remember the story, and everyone would also remember Grandpa Eddie did whatever it took to help his customer have the best experience possible.

Take a look at the origin narrative that my conversation with Jenny eventually produced for Charnecke Tents.

The Problems of the Day Were Forgotten.

In the year 1929, in a small town in Wisconsin, the economic problems of the day weighed heavily. But one night, there was a party. A big one. Ed Charnecke, the founder of Charnecke

Tents, led the revelry as a pair of newlyweds celebrated with friends and family.

Grandpa Eddie—ever resourceful—furnished a large canvas tent he'd purchased as a business opportunity. He provided the entertainment (he played his concertina in a local polka band—Rhythm Kings) and even supplied his own home-brewed moonshine.

A business was born.

Couples would not only rent a tent for their big day, but would gladly enjoy the "package deal" of: renting the polka band, tables, chairs and dance floor. For those homesteads living in remote rural areas, Ed could furnish a generator for electricity and moonshine for sheer enjoyment!

Ed certainly capitalized on his ingenuity as a businessman; he understood the value of "add-on sales," because he created that business model! This method enabled him to provide for his family, thereby surviving the Great Depression.

In the late 1970s, son Ken Charnecke Sr. joined the rental business. Similar traits and talents combined with broader vision for the company's future, Ken decided to make his own tents capable of servicing many events throughout the state on any given weekend or special occasion. All of this exposure was ambitious and popular…ultimately leading us to develop into the manufacturing company we are today.

We proudly continue our traditions instilled by generations before us. Our family-run business includes both children of Ken Sr.: Ken Charnecke Jr. and Jenny Cole. We commit ourselves to not only providing high-quality Charnecke Tents manufactured on-site with additional celebration rental equipment to our newest expansion of providing a means to wash tents. CCC Washers is our sister company; born from a long-standing tradition of inventiveness, hard work and family pride.

I invite you to take a close look at this origin narrative, modeled broadly on FedEx's but utterly different from it, and consider how well it accomplishes the same objectives.

- It shares a classic storytelling archetype—in this case, the *likeable outlaw*. (Think Butch Cassidy and the Sundance Kid.) Again, people buy into classic archetypes!

- In using that archetype, it gives us a memorable incident that explains why, when, and how Charnecke Tents was founded—one that is fun to share with other people. How can you forget about a company founded by grandpa, the moonshiner and bootlegger?

- It tells us exactly what Charnecke Tents does best.

- It sets up two concepts that are integral elements of the company's brand promise: *the tradition of going the extra mile* and *family.* These are critical themes because they appeal to Charnecke's "moose"—families who want the very best environment for an important celebration. Notice that this "moose" is *not* primarily focused on securing the cheapest price for a tent but on creating the highest quality experience. The themes of *tradition, family,* and *putting the customer first* let prospective customers know that a) Charnecke is a family-operated company dedicated to quality and b) it has been in the business a very long time and knows how to take the best possible care of its customers.

- Its origin story is memorable and sharable! "Yes, we are using Charnecke Tents. The owners' grandfather started the company back in the Depression and, yep, he was a bootlegger!"

I'm happy to be able to report Charnecke's sales rose dramatically after their marketing campaign embraced this origin narrative as its central element. This gives you some idea of the potential power and impact of Stealing Genius Level 1!

COUNTLESS APPLICATIONS

Of course, your objective may not have anything to do with marketing your business. You can harness the power of innovation to improve virtually *any* process and solve virtually *any* problem your team—your INNOVATION COALITION—happens to be faced with. But you must first define your objective!

Sometimes this takes a fair amount of discussion. Sometimes it doesn't. Very often, people in the coalition already have a pretty clear idea of the problem they're trying to solve. A while back, I was working with executives at the Golf Course Superintendents Association of America (GCSAA), who were designing their annual trade show. Their goal, already pretty clearly defined by the time they reached out to me, was to get attendees to come in contact with as many of the exhibitors who were paying for display space at the show. It's a difficult situation when you're charging exhibitors for space and they find themselves stuck in an unpopular aisle of the venue where hardly anyone is passing by! So the question became, *How do we design the floor plan of the trade show in such a way as to ensure maximum exposure for all of the exhibitors?* That was our objective.

Naturally, our next step was to ask: *What alien organization is really, really good at consciously designing foot traffic flow?*

What alien organization is really, really good at doing what you want to do?

We came up with *two* relevant answers—two powerful alien influences we could draw on to develop an innovative approach to solving this problem. In fact, I am sharing this story because it's important for you to know you can *combine* alien influences as you and your coalition are innovating. I should also point out that in this case, as in all the other innovation campaigns I've helped out with, we looked at dozens of possible aliens we could emulate before we settled on the plan that made the most sense. In this case, there were two alien influences.

The first one we studied was the great American supermarket. Is the supermarket industry the same as the trade show industry? Actually, yes. It is a large marketplace where thousands of products (exhibitors) are vying for the attention of buyers (attendees) walking the aisles. The store wants to get those consumers to cover as much of the floor as they can, right? Did it have something to *teach* us about the management of foot traffic? Absolutely.

Think about it. There are plenty of times when a shopper steps into the supermarket and is not aiming to buy a long list of items. In fact, it's quite common for people to stop into the supermarket to get just *one* item—say, a gallon of milk. And yet, to *reach* the milk you always have to navigate multiple aisles, don't you? Guess what? That's no accident. The people who design supermarkets make a point of putting things like milk, bread, and other staples either all the way in the back or at the far side of the store—a long way from the entrance. Of course, they *could* put milk and bread—the two most likely purchases for people aiming to get in and out quickly—right near the entrance. But they never do. They always make you take a little trip through the store in order to get to that product they know you need. Things like milk and bread basically serve as magnets that draw you through other parts of the store. So that design choice from the world of supermarkets got us thinking: *What if we created a magnet of our own—something that would draw people through the exhibit hall, following a course we designed?*

That question pointed us toward our second alien influence: Walt Disney. Disney was famous for designing his theme parks around something he oddly called "the weenie." That was Disney's playful term for an attraction that is, in the words of Disney insiders, "big enough to be seen from a distance and interesting enough to make you want to take a closer look." The classic example of a weenie in the Disney theme-park realm is Cinderella's Castle, which can be found at the end of Main Street, USA at Walt Disney World. Think of the weenie as a visual inducement to keep walking, keep seeing, keep experiencing, keep being "pulled" in its direction. If the weenie is interesting enough and placed strategically enough, it becomes the heart of the physical space. It sets the terms for the journey, like that gallon of milk you walked into the supermarket to buy—but unlike the gallon of milk, it's both exciting and visible from a distance, thanks to the "hub-and-spoke" design employed at Disney theme parks.

Combining these two alien influences, we were able to put together a plan for innovation. We would draw people through the hall in pursuit of a specific goal, just like the people who designed supermarkets did. And we would forget about the traditional parallel aisle design typically used at trade shows. Instead, we would deploy a hub-and-spoke design, with a compelling attraction in the middle, like the designers of the Disney theme parks did.

What was that compelling attraction? We knew golf course superintendents love dirt. Every day they're up before dawn caring for their 7,000 yards. They're mowing fairways and greens. They're raking and shaping sand traps. They might be fixing a broken water line in the morning and trimming trees that afternoon. They take great pride in their work. And like I said, they love dirt.

We ended up actually building, from scratch, right in the center of that trade show venue, a fully functional golfing green, complete with real grass and two sand traps! Trucks came in with dirt, sand, and all the building materials, and a crew went to work, building a section of a real golf course right there on the concrete floor. This was a major project, and fascinating to watch, especially for golf course superintendents (the moose).

It took three days to set up, but we staggered that timing quite consciously so people attending the trade show could see this remarkable exhibit being installed over the first three days, get excited about it, talk about it, and then get in line to play on it on day four! Which was exactly what happened. There was heavy competition for tee times.

Long story short: the "weenie" idea was a sensation. Everyone in attendance, it seemed, made a point of checking out the indoor green. The superintendents repeatedly returned to the construction site to see the progress. And thanks to the hub-and-spoke layout, everyone got a chance to check out exhibitors who had bought booth space along the various pathways that *led* to the indoor green!

This was a big innovation win. I chalked it up to the American supermarket, to Walt Disney World, and, most important of all, to a willingness to create a clear objective—and then look high and low to find out who is world-class when it comes to attaining that objective.

Postscript: It was a total pain to make happen. Convention centers aren't designed for hub-and-spoke arrangements, or any original ideas for managing traffic flow. That was the one and only year we broke the rules. But for that one year, despite the difficulty, the GCSAA pulled off an amazing feat that people are still talking about. We built a real, playable green with sand traps on the concrete floor of a convention center in three days.

DO YOU NEED TO REVIEW YOUR ASSUMPTIONS?

Warning: The problem may not be what you think it is.

This Stealing Genius technique sometimes reveals an assumption that's been built into your organization's major objectives that may not be worth holding on to. Case in point: A manufacturing client I am working with needed some help with a question that had a major impact on multiple processes inside the organization: *What is the problem most likely to motivate prospective customers to decide to work with us?*

Sometimes, an assumption that has been built into your major business strategy is not worth holding on to.

The answer to this question not only affected team objectives in sales and marketing, as you might expect—it also affected objectives in operations, R&D, and accounting, all of whom were responsible for supplying information and resources that *supported* sales and marketing. For years, executives at this company had assumed they already knew the answer to this question. They told me the answer was as follows: *Customers work with us because they want to be more efficient. Our state-of-the-art machinery is far more productive than the competition's, and because of its superior design, it will help them to produce more stuff, faster and cheaper.*

The problem was, it was a harder sale than they expected.

Like many, if not most, companies, my client looked at their sales messaging from the "look at how much more efficient, faster, and cheaper you'll be able to produce" perspective. Many of their moose responded with, "But my current machines are all paid for. Why do I want to take on such a large debt right now when I'm less than ten years away from selling my business?"

After several conversations, my client and I realized he needed to come at this problem from a different angle. Instead of marketing the benefits of buying his state-of-the-art machinery, we needed to find a big pain point for the moose. We needed a new Stealing Genius Level 1 objective.

Once we flipped our thinking, it didn't take long. The moose were telling us they were looking ahead to selling their businesses and retiring. More than one would say something along the line of, "I want to sell out, take my big check, and go retire on my boat in Florida."

BINGO! That gave us a new objective. Was there anything that could happen between now and then to prevent them from getting a big check? That would create a potentially painful scenario for my client's moose.

Discussions with an alien resource, a financial professional, confirmed my suspicions. The machinery my client offered, he said, was going to be seen as a major investment, one requiring a loan from the bank to purchase, by people who had *already* bought equipment long ago that did the same job, equipment that was now paid for in full. They wouldn't owe any money on the current equipment, and as far as the customer is concerned, that equipment worked fine. They were likely to hang on to the equipment they had until it broke down and had to be replaced, which, they felt, would be long after they sold out.

In my discussions with this financial pro, however, I learned about a whole *new* business problem for the decision-makers my client was targeting: selling their business at a profit.

Very often, I learned, business owners in the market that my client was targeting shockingly found, when it came time to talk about selling their company, that their company was worth far less than they were expecting. The many-years-old machinery that currently cranked out products for sale would not be seen as high-valued assets, as their lifespan was rapidly declining and they would soon need to be replaced. We realized one possibility to drive the future value of the company up: set up a plan to install top-of-the line factory equipment! The equipment purchase thus became part of a long-term *strategic planning* discussion about creating an exit strategy, as opposed to addressing an efficiency issue.

We never would have found that out if I hadn't challenged one of the core assumptions driving the organization's objectives, talked about it with someone outside the "box" my client was used to operating in, and asked some questions that had not yet been asked.

WHAT IF YOU DON'T KNOW
WHAT YOUR OBJECTIVE IS?

Often, I will work with people who know they want to innovate. They are having a hard time differentiating themselves from the competition. Everything they do is quickly copied by competitors. They don't know what to do next. They're not sure they're looking at the right objectives. Sometimes, as in the story I just shared with you, they've latched onto assumptions that may need to be questioned. If you fall into this category, it's quite possible you're wondering if there is a step in the Stealing Genius process designed just for you.

There is. It's the second Stealing Genius level: *Look Outside Your Industry to Organizations You Admire.* And it's covered in the next chapter.

THE BIG TAKEAWAY:

Assemble an Innovation Coalition, challenge existing assumptions as necessary, and get consensus on the specific problem you need to solve.

DO THIS:

It's time to determine whom, specifically, you are hoping to serve through your innovation, as well as the specific nature of the challenge you are facing.

First, make sure you know your "moose" by answering the following questions:

- Who is your moose?
- How do they behave?
- What kind of moose bait are you using?

Second, create your own "What Are We Trying to Fix" narrative by defining the value you deliver (X), the high-priority problem (Y), and the action you must take (Z) to solve the problem using that value.

Identify alien organizations that are really, really good at what you want to do.

Now that you know what you are trying to fix, commit the necessary time, attention, and financial and human resources necessary to innovate and solve the problem.

GET THE "STEALING GENIUS FIELD GUIDE" PLUS MORE USEFUL INFORMATION AND TIPS! GO TO:

stealinggenius.com/resources

Ideas for Stealing Genius

CH 3

STEALING GENIUS LEVEL 2: LOOK OUTSIDE YOUR INDUSTRY TO ORGANIZATIONS YOU ADMIRE

"We need role models who are going to break the mold."
—Carly Simon

The second technique of Stealing Genius is to find an organization that inspires you and then look closely, and at length, at what that organization does right that could be adapted to your world. You don't have to have a specific objective in mind. This level looks for the "AHA!" moment when you discover something unexpected you can steal.

There are a few important preconditions to bear in mind here before you start thinking about how you will go about selecting the organization you will be looking at.

- Firstly, the organization you choose to study closely must operate entirely *outside* of your industry or field of endeavor, i.e., in a completely different box.

- Secondly, the organization you choose to study must have demonstrated a long period of success in its own chosen field. Flashy start-ups and cool new ideas are fascinating, and you can sometimes gain interesting insights from studying them, but that is not the kind of undertaking we are talking about here. What we're talking about is identifying an organization that has proven itself, over time, to be among the leaders and forward thinkers in its field. You are looking for best practices from best-in-class teams and organizations.

- Thirdly, bear in mind this technique is reserved for people and teams who might be struggling with the first one I shared with you. In other words, you should build this step into your process if you either *don't know what business objective you should be focusing your innovation on…* or you *suspect some of the assumptions guiding your current objectives may be off base.* Either way, if you're open to the possibility of identifying some new assumptions, some new objectives, and some new opportunities, Level 2 is for you.

OPENING UP NEW HORIZONS

The sociologist and philosopher Erich Fromm once observed, "Creativity requires the courage to let go of certainty." That sentence captures the essence of what we are doing here in Level 2 of the Stealing Genius process. We are setting aside all of our certainties, even the certainty of having a specific goal. And for a lot of people, this takes a measure of courage. If it helps, consider that you will not be abandoning your certainties, your specialties, and your hard-won experience forever. You will just be putting them away for a short while—so you can get a glimpse of what excellence looks like in an entirely different realm than the one in which you are used to operating; so you can discover a new kind of genius you can steal.

It is best to begin this process with senior leadership fully committed to the undertaking and personally taking part in it. That helps others in the organization make the decision to commit time, resources, and attention to the task of finding an organization everyone admires, either from direct experience or through the accounts of third parties who have bought from or worked with that organization.

This is what happened when Caterpillar Inc., the legendary construction machinery and equipment company, asked for help in building innovation more deeply into their culture and their daily operations. Several senior members of the organization told me they wanted to take part in a program that would make innovation more of a priority at Caterpillar. I made it clear at the outset that what I had in mind was much more than a series of sober discussions around a conference table. What I had in mind was opening up entirely new horizons—and moving beyond old certainties. This process, I told the team, would not only require them to rebuild their boxes…it would require them to get out of their offices. Eventually, once we had boiled down our "long list" of possible organizations we wanted to study to a "short list" of one, we would be hitting the road to see exactly how that team operated—first-hand.

But before we could do that, of course, we had to figure out who belonged on the list! This brings me to the very first thing you want to do in Level 2, which is…

Generate a list of cool companies and organizations you admire.

They can come from anywhere…any industry…B2B and B2C. These can be companies you've bought stuff from, companies your friends or family members have bought stuff from, companies you've heard consistently good things about, nonprofits whose mission and track record inspire you, rock bands you've seen on tour and enjoyed—you name it. This is a fascinating exercise, one that will tell you all kinds of interesting things about the people in your Innovation Coalition. Your job in this first step is simple: make the list as long as possible. Just make sure you don't include any direct or indirect competitors of your organization, and remember that your focus is on *companies and organizations*, not individuals.

Generate a list of cool companies and organizations you admire.

As you and the rest of the group put together your list, don't just jot down any old company. Make sure you are picking truly inspiring operations. One way to do that is to raise (and take notes on) the following questions for every proposed candidate:

- What makes this organization different?

- What makes this organization cool?

- What makes this organization successful?

- What do I love about this organization?

- Is this organization a rule-breaker?

- Is this organization a rule-maker?

If people don't have great answers to any of these questions, cross the organization off the list!

This part of the process can be very lively. For at least an hour, or longer if you can, just keep adding candidates to the list and taking your initial notes on those candidates—as long as you continue hearing plausible answers to those six questions.

Very often, companies get put on the list because one individual knows about that company and has great stories to tell about it—but no one else has ever heard of the firm. So a small local outfit with a great product or service, a great group of people, and a great working culture ends up making it onto the list—and who knows, may even end up being one of the aliens the group chooses to study closely and Steal Genius from! I mention this because I like to encourage this kind of thing. There is nothing wrong with putting big companies with great, wide-reaching reputations on your list. It's very common to see firms like Apple, Zappos, and Herman Miller enter the conversation. But try to ensure your long list has some balance to it by including a few smaller entities, too. And again, don't be afraid to place an organization on the list that operates in a space that is as far as imaginable from what you do! The more names like that that you can add, the better.

One good way to be prepared for these types of meetings is to keep a "Swipe File." This can be digital or analog, whichever you like best. Whenever you come across a very interesting example of an Uncopyable organization, write it down and put it in your Swipe File. Take pictures. Copy articles. Collect as much evidence of alien genius thinking as you can. The next time you do an exercise like Level 2, you'll have a collection of idea starters.

For example, I often receive emails from my BFFs[1] sharing stories about Uncopyable organizations ripe for stealing genius from. Just yesterday, one of my BFFs alerted me to a great example, GORUCK. I'll let Justin tell the story:

One such company that has really captured the essence of what you are talking about is GORUCK. Maybe you have never heard of them, but that's perhaps because you aren't looking for expensive, high-end, military style backpacks. In any case, the marketing job they did is second to none in that industry and has made me, and then by extension my personal friends also, customers of their brand. The amazing thing is I didn't even start becoming their customer by purchasing any of their gear but rather through the experience they create.

GORUCK was founded by an Army veteran who wanted a better rucksack (backpack) to stand up to the extreme elements he had experienced as a Special Forces operator. Also, he wanted it made 100% in the USA. He did end up creating this, and it comes with a high price due to the higher quality and American manufacturing. To prove the quality of his product the owner created events known as GORUCK events where people sign up to experience tortures similar to the indoctrination phase that a typical Special Forces candidate would experience. He actually hired veterans of Special Forces groups to run the events known as GORUCK challenges.

As you can imagine, many crazy people like me are eager to prove themselves in such a challenge. The genius part is a participant is not required to use the GORUCK brand backpack. You are required to use a backpack of some sort and must carry certain provisions, such as a 15–30-pound weight depending on your size, but it need not be the GORUCK brand. I myself did not use a GORUCK pack in my first event.

As you have likely predicted at this point, the conclusion of such events ends up creating more GORUCK customers. Not only are event participants impressed by the quality of the product, but they are also eager to join the cult. Carrying a GORUCK pack comes with a certain amount of pride. In fact, I ran across another GORUCK customer in one of my daily hikes around a local park while carrying my pack, and we stopped and spoke to one another for some time happily discussing our experiences with GORUCK. I would never have done this over any other backpack brand before.

I'm not sure whether or not GORUCK ever hired you for marketing consulting, but they certainly seem to understand your Uncopyable message. I will strive for the same if I ever create my own brand someday.

Sincerely,

Justin Kane

This is what I encouraged the team at Caterpillar to do. They followed my lead. They started talking about companies they or their family members really loved and had great experiences with. And so in addition to companies like Apple, Zappos, and Herman Miller, we added a name to the list no one at Caterpillar could have predicted ahead of time would serve as an effective role model for a global manufacturer of tractors and construction equipment vehicles: the American Girl store. (If you're not sure what that is, keep reading. Everything will become clear shortly.)

WINNOW DOWN THE LIST

At some point, you will return to your "long list" with the aim of turning it into a "short list." The goal here is to cross companies off the list, intelligently and with the consensus of the group, so the list gets stronger and stronger in terms of the potential role models it offers to the group. Eventually, you want to be looking at a list that is only one or two names long.

Cross names off the list.

The notes you took during Step 1 will come in handy during this step. Review those notes closely, and you should start to notice certain patterns emerging when it comes to *group* enthusiasm for certain organizations. Remember: As people added their ideas to the list, they were supposed to back up their suggestions by saying specifically what was *different* about the outfit they were nominating, what was *cool* about them, what made them *successful*, and what they *loved* about that organization. When one of those answers energized the group and got people excited, someone (you, if you're the one taking notes) should have noticed that enthusiasm and placed a star by whatever it was that created a moment of agreement. Whenever a company or organization under discussion got the members of the group shaking their heads and thinking, "That is the direction we want to go," you want to identify what elicited that response and place a star by it.

I should also point out that several, if not all, of the organizations on your final list should make many of you a bit uncomfortable. New ideas should not be comfortable! If your examples don't make you squirm a bit, then they're not different enough.

Now, in Step 2, you are going to notice where those stars are and start a discussion about which should be the highest priority for identifying an alien resource you want to study closely. You want to find out what energizes the group, what excites your Innovation Coalition and inspires discussion. That which inspires discussion and engagement has the potential to inspire action. So those are the companies you want to keep on your list. Try to boil down what people liked about each "starred" company to a single sentence. Then have a discussion about which of those aspects is the highest priority for your Innovation Coalition moving forward.

For instance, in the discussions with Caterpillar, people responded positively to three very different companies, for three wildly different reasons:

- Apple, for its commitment to creativity in designing and marketing its products.

- Zappos, for its extraordinary commitment to the customer.

- The American Girl store, for its ability to forge strong emotional attachments with its customers.

In the end, we decided that forging a strong emotional attachment was the most important priority for Caterpillar. And so we chose the one-of-a-kind retail operation known as the American Girl store as the alien influence from which we would be Stealing Genius.

HIT THE ROAD

The third and arguably most important step of this process is to physically visit the organization you have selected.

It is not enough to Google them, not enough to swap stories, not enough to order something online. You want to get a *first-hand* look at the workings of the operation, and ideally you want to do this all together. Making the trip *as a team* is an essential part of what you're doing here, because the act of getting out of your familiar physical space and visiting a different physical environment is an essential trigger for getting out of your familiar *mental* space and creating new approaches to the challenges and opportunities you face. So: Call the organization in question. If necessary, set up a time to tour the offices, plant, or store. The entire Innovation Coalition must make the trip as a team activity. Think of this as a field trip with the destination of Innovation!

Go on a field trip.

The Caterpillar team I was working with was (and is) based in Peoria, Illinois; the American Girl store we had decided to visit was (and is) based in Chicago. Caterpillar was fully committed to the goal of raising their company's game in terms of innovation, and they had allocated the resources necessary to make that trip. So when we were winnowing down our short list, we knew a trip to Chicago made sense for this particular team. However, your company may not have the resources allocated to make that kind of trip, in which case you will want to take factors like travel costs, logistics, and hotel accommodations into account as you winnow down your list. You might have to arrange for some new, creative way to "tour" your target organization. In our case, though, the costs for the trip made sense—and I will go a little further and say that they were a positive factor in getting the Caterpillar team out of their customary mental "box." Why do I say that? Because all the executives who had committed to this trip knew they were spending a significant amount of money on it, and they were, as a result, focused intently on getting their money's worth…which they certainly did.

It makes sense now for me to give you a little background information about the American Girl store we visited. The Chicago store was the first of its kind, and it was for some years the sole inspiration for a remarkable kind of family trip, a trip made by countless families over the years. It is what you might call an "event destination." Going there with your family means a lot more than, say, going to the mall or ordering something online. This is a trip that can be compared to a kind of family pilgrimage.

Our family made our first such pilgrimage when Kelly turned ten years old. Several weeks before, I'd asked what she wanted for her "big 1-0." Without hesitation, she said, "I want to go to the American Girl store."

At that time, there was only one American Girl store—in Chicago. But I had plenty of airline and hotel points, so our "pilgrimage" was given the green light.

Please understand why I would use a word like that to describe a journey to someone unfamiliar with the American Girl phenomenon. That person might be tempted to describe it, inaccurately, as "a trip to a doll store." I would suggest you talk to a girl in your family between the ages of, say, seven and eleven. The odds are good she will be able to fill you in about everything that makes American Girl dolls different from other dolls and about why a trip to an American Girl store is worth making, no matter where you happen to live. If you don't happen to have such a person in your family, and you are not yet up to speed on the powerful and extraordinary appeal of the American Girl line of dolls and their related products, just bear in mind this is not merely a place where you can go to buy dolls and doll accessories. This is a place where you can take your American Girl doll to get her ears pierced. This is a place where you can go to an American Girl-themed cafe and order items off the menu that connect with your favorite stories and characters. This is a place where you can have a birthday party you'll remember for the rest of your life. This is a place where you can immerse yourself in new themed environments and get your hair and nails done—at the same time your American Girl doll is getting hers done! In short, this really is an "event destination." Back when we took Kelly to its original Chicago location, they had large restaurant with a six-month waiting list and a Broadway-caliber theater!

Thanks in no small degree to the extraordinary consumer experience offered at the American Girl store, these dolls—which have launched successful movie and TV projects—are now part of the country's cultural landscape. But what lies at the foundation of this brand? What drives all the seemingly unquenchable interest in the American Girl product line, which has to be one of most remarkable and enduring success stories in the history of the US toy industry? That's what we went to Chicago to find out.

Each of the classic American Girl dolls tells the story of a girl from a particular period of American history. Each doll is accompanied by a carefully crafted, beautifully designed book that relates that story, in age-appropriate and reading-level-appropriate terms, from the point of view of the girl represented by the doll. Each doll has its own line of clothes and accessories, keyed to the historical timeframe and character details of the protagonist.

To date, the stores have welcomed over 94 million visitors (which puts American Girl retail outlets in the same conversation with destinations like Disneyland and the Washington Monument), and over 157 million dolls have been sold—at what can only be described as premium prices. As of this writing, a standard American Girl doll and book set retails for around $110! And note you cannot buy a classic American Girl doll without the accompanying book!

The key to all the extraordinary (and high-margin!) customer loyalty is the brand's ability to *engage girls and their families emotionally* via the story of each American Girl protagonist drawn from a particular period of history.[2] This is what has kept girls and families coming back to the website, and to the American Girl store, in extraordinary numbers. The over-the-top sales numbers, for products set well above the supposed "price point" of either a doll or a book offered separately, are possible because the doll and the book, together, constitute a product that appeals to girls on an emotional level. During our visit, I asked a manager, "What's your secret? How do you get entire families to do this over and over again?" She smiled and said, "We put vitamins in the cake. The cake is the play value and the emotional connection with the doll. The vitamins are the historical accuracy of the story. The cake appeals to the kids. The vitamins appeal to the parents and grandparents."

This brand has resonated on a mass scale with not one, not two, but three successive generations of young girls in the United States: Millennials (born 1980–1995), Gen Z (1996–2009), and Gen Alpha (2010–2025). That third cohort, of course, is still being born…but don't bet against the American Girl store's ability to continue to connect emotionally with this emerging target demographic!

Consider this 2015 observation from a (now-grown-up) fan of the American Girl experience:

"The books were actually good." That is a direct quote from my mom. A lot of movies and books for children…are mind-numbingly boring for adults, but kids and their parents can get invested in the American Girl books, which are smart and emotionally resonant. Reading about the challenges faced by people in different historical eras is a great way to generate conversations amongst families…. I think it is especially important that, at least in the case of the historical line, these dolls are distinct, fully fledged characters. Addy is not "African American Barbie"—i.e., simply a black version of a white character. She has her own story, her own clothes and accessories, and her own personality. She is a fully realized, unique character who is valuable in her own right. And I think this is the message of the American Girl Dolls more generally: Girls, regardless of when and where they are born, have agency. They are unique and worthwhile. They matter.[3]

Mattel, the giant of the industry, currently operates by means of three divisions: North America, International…and American Girl! This iconic brand is now estimated to deliver over $100 million in gross revenue each year, but such figures do not give a complete picture of the engagement and interaction that happens at the consumer level, which is where the emotional bonds are forged. For that, you need to visit the stores themselves.

Before we stepped into the store, I said to the Caterpillar executives: "I challenge you to go in there and look at this place from a purely clinical point of view. Imagine you're wearing a white coat and you have a clipboard. You're on a research team. Don't do anything other than observe what's happening—and ask yourselves, *How does this store make money? Why do they do it that way?*

Here's what we saw:

We saw parents and grandparents—dozens of them, hundreds of them—getting closer to their daughters and granddaughters, sharing an experience that wasn't just about right now, but one the family would *continue to share*, not just on the ride home, but for years to come. We saw families coming together. What had made that remarkable level of connection possible? It was pretty obvious to me. The connection those families were experiencing was the direct result of the power of the *narratives*. And *history.*

We saw parents and kids talking excitedly about the *stories* that had been carefully developed around classic American Girl characters like Addy Walker, Kit Kittredge, Felicity Merriman (Kelly's doll), Samantha Parkington, and Molly McIntyre. These weren't "dolls" the girls and their families were engaged with. They were *people*, quite real in the moment to those girls. Each American Girl protagonist brought her own distinctive outlook, obstacles, struggles, and lessons learned from a particular period of her personal history—and America's history. And because those resonated with customers, each character's story became an important part of the lives of the girls and families we saw before us. That's what happens when you get people engaged with *stories* that truly make a difference to them. They take them on!

We saw parents laughing right out loud with their daughters, thanks to the skillful *narrative* that had brought those characters to life for each and every girl in that store. We saw parents smiling at their daughters' reactions to each new historically accurate American Girl outfit, each new historically accurate accessory, each new story, each new adventure—and all of those smiles and all of that laughter, we realized, was thanks to the power of *emotional engagement*. Not only that—we saw that every single time a parent made a deeper emotional connection with a daughter…that family made a deep emotional connection with the American Girl brand. All of it was due to the power of narrative, of storytelling, with a historical focus.

And we saw families *leaving* the American Girl store who looked absolutely ecstatic. Happy that they had made the pilgrimage. Happy to have made their (large!) purchases. And happy to have spent time together in such a special place.

Talk about engagement! Talk about interaction!

Now, this is not just what *I* saw as we watched families interact at the American Girl store. This is what every single member of the Innovation Coalition saw for themselves first-hand. And I really don't think the lesson we all learned about the power of narrative would have had quite the visceral impact it did if we hadn't all seen it in person.

I should mention here that one of the Caterpillar executives' concerns—one of the reasons they had decided in the first place to work with me on innovation—was they were concerned about how they engaged with end users: drivers and operators. They were looking for something other than price to distinguish themselves in the market. They were concerned about something a lot of business leaders are concerned about: commoditization. They were looking for attachment.

At one point during our visit, I took all the Caterpillar executives aside, gestured to a family that was at the checkout counter, buying a large amount of American Girl merchandise, and asked them: "How much price sensitivity do you see on those faces?"

We all knew the answer: *None.*

That was the point from which we began: the experience in the store had been so impactful, and had connected families so strongly to the American Girl brand, that price was really not a factor in any of the purchases. As a practical matter, for these families, American Girl did not compete for mind share or wallet share with any other toy or book purchase. American Girl was something the family *did* that had the daughter at the center of the experience. They really weren't competing with other doll manufacturers. They had built their own box.

Later, back at headquarters, we debriefed. We all agreed the chief driver behind the extraordinary emotional connection girls and their families had with the American Girl brand could be traced to two closely overlapping factors: *narrative* and *history.* And the conclusion the executives eventually reached—the genius they stole—was the proposition that Caterpillar could engage emotionally with its customers in a similarly powerful, in-person way.

EXECUTE!

The next step is to take an idea you've picked up from your alien influence—the bigger the better—and then set up and implement a plan for its execution. Again, bear in mind the whole purpose of this level is to take you, your team, and your organization outside of your comfort zone, outside of the assumptions and preconceived notions you have built up by doing business in the way you have grown accustomed to doing it. If the idea you've latched onto feels familiar, feels safe, feels like some variation of what you have been doing up to this point, *go back to the drawing board.* Your goal is to adopt the *mindset* of your alien influence, at the same time as you are adopting *best practices*, and both should be a bit uncomfortable, personally and organizationally. If it does not make you uncomfortable, you're not stretching enough!

Of course, the main thing the Caterpillar executives wanted to do was what American Girl had so masterfully done: build their own box for engaging with end users. I believe engagement equals attachment. We looked at a number of different ways of doing that. Most importantly, perhaps, the executives started *thinking* differently about engaging with their end users!

Take the big ideas from your field trip that pull you outside of your comfort zone, ask how you can adapt (steal) them— and execute.

I can't say I had direct impact with certainty, but a while after I left the discussion about creating attachment with end users, Caterpillar created their own version of the American Girl store—an "event destination" that was distinctively theirs, one that told the extraordinary true story of Caterpillar's major role in the building and feeding of America. This idea eventually became the Caterpillar Museum and Visitor Center, which you can visit today in Peoria, Illinois.

You may not have thought of a tractor company creating a tourist attraction, but that is exactly what Caterpillar executives did, modeling what we all saw first-hand at the American Girl store in Chicago: *engagement.*

A trip to this place is also a pilgrimage of sorts, one that celebrates, not just the company, but a powerful and memorable narrative, namely, the modern agricultural and industrial history of the United States. Here's a brief overview:

Your experience begins with a video in the bed of a massive two-and-a-half story Cat® 797F Mining Truck as you take a virtual ride into a customer's mine site down a haul road.

Unleash your inner engineer and design your very own Cat machine. Hop onto a simulator and see first-hand what it's like to operate equipment the way our operators do.

See what the Holt steam track-type tractor prototype from 1905 looked like. Get up close and personal with the first Caterpillar-engineered machine—the Model Twenty. Sit in the seat of an antique Caterpillar D8 Tractor and feel what it was like to operate this machine in the 1930s....

When is a doll store not a doll store? When it's engaging, a reason for a family pilgrimage, thus creating attachment. When is an earth mover not an earth mover? When it's history you're engaging with first-hand, with your family by your side!

MOVING BEYOND THE "UGLY GIRLFRIEND" TEST

Let's look at another great example of the second level of Stealing Genius. If you haven't yet seen the film *Moneyball* (based on the fine book by Michael Lewis), it's likely you at least know two things about it: a) it stars Brad Pitt, and b) it's about baseball. Given those two facts, you'd be forgiven for imagining this is another sports movie about a team of lovable underdogs who face down a nasty on-field and/or off-field adversary, overcome clubhouse problems, learn to work together, and win the World Series at the end of the film. Actually, this is *not* that kind of movie. It's the true story of how Oakland A's general manager

Billy Beane implemented Level 2 of Stealing Genius during the 2002 Major League Baseball season.

Spoiler alert: The A's didn't win the World Series that year. But under Beane's leadership, the A's front office did something that in the long run might well have been even more important than winning a championship: they upended the way Major League Baseball assembled competitive teams. They did that by stepping outside of their own, familiar box; building a whole new box; and looking at things from the point of view of an alien organization. In this case, that organization was the economics department of Harvard University.

That's where Beane's assistant general manager in real life, Paul DePodesta, got his college degree. And Harvard was basically what Beane hired when he brought DePodesta to the A's. DePodesta (who eventually became a general manager in the big leagues in his own right) got the A's job because Beane knew he could be counted on to *think* like the Harvard economics major he was. DePodesta was, and is, all about the numbers, a habit that ruffled feathers at some staff meetings.

DePodesta took a very different approach to staffing decisions than most baseball professionals of the time did. He focused more on the data and the analytical tools available to him to answer specific questions…and less on intangible, subjective factors, like whether a player had a "classic swing" or a "baseball body," or was "ready to play the part," or (I swear I am not making this up) was confident enough to be in a relationship with a sufficiently attractive woman. No joke: the seasoned baseball men on Beane's staff took factors like whether a player had an "ugly girlfriend" very seriously indeed when making signing recommendations! Such clichés and generalizations, which really had driven major signing decisions in the past in Oakland, were deeply rooted in the approaches of traditional baseball scouting and personnel approaches. Beane was uninterested in those traditions.

Beane wanted the A's to get out of their box. Beane wanted help from Harvard. He wanted to know how the world's best numbers guys analyzed data so he could make better choices.

By insisting the A's model their thinking on the economics department at an Ivy League university, rather than on the thinking that had gotten them to the dismal spot they occupied, Beane and DePodesta formed a partnership that shook things up. They infuriated their own manager, who tried and failed to subvert the team they designed. They stayed the course.

They didn't just get out of their box; they built a new box. As a result, they laid the groundwork for a revolution in talent assessment in big-league baseball—and oh, yes, despite having one of the smallest budgets for payroll in the major leagues, put together a record-setting 20-game winning streak and won a division they had been predicted to lose. Footnote: Two years later, the Boston Red Sox won the 2004 World Series using basically the same statistical model of talent deployment developed by Bean and DePodesta. And it had nothing to do with talent scouts sitting around a table talking about how attractive a player's girlfriend was.

Set up a new game, with new rules.

Just as the Caterpillar executives chose to look at a role model from well beyond their area of specialty in order to move beyond their comfort zone, Beane *recruited* someone who was schooled in an entirely different discipline—economics—in order to take the A's out of their box. And in so doing, he not only changed the way the Athletics operated; he changed baseball forever. He built his own box. He set up a whole new game, with a whole new set of rules, and he forced everyone else to try to keep up.

LOOK FOR A DIFFERENT EXPERT!

We all get used to listening to the acknowledged experts in our departments, our organizations, and our industries. Sometimes those experts have good insights to offer. But sometimes they get trapped by their own knowledge (i.e., they are operating in a familiar box!). And when they do, we need to find a different voice to listen to, a different set of experts to inspire us, a different role model to follow. Otherwise, we may find ourselves accepting received wisdom that has no more going for it than the sage advice that we sign the ballplayer with the most attractive girlfriend!

I used to be a professional golfer. And so I know a lot of golfers and a lot of golf teachers. For many, many years, I saw golf teachers pass along the same received wisdom that had been circulating for years, without even bothering to check whether it was relevant to the person they were teaching. I'd meet pros all over the place, and I would see a golf pro take somebody out to the driving range for a lesson. And that person would be big—say, six-foot-three, 220 pounds. And the golf pro would say: "Okay, now the key to you being successful is that when you get to the top of your swing, you want to be pulling down with your left hand. That's what you want to do." And then the next day I would see that same pro working with a woman who was maybe five-foot-three and 130 pounds. And I would hear him say the exact same thing: "Okay, now the key to you being successful in your game is as follows: when you get to the top of your swing, you want to be pulling down with your left hand. That's what you want to do." They would teach that to everybody, whether it was relevant to the individual golfer or not! And I knew that very often, it wasn't!

Sometimes we need to stop and ask ourselves: Is the received wisdom really all that wise, or even relevant? Is it the same common advice we might hear from other "experts" inside our box? And if not, who else could we be listening to?

THE BIG TAKEAWAY:

Shake things up. Identify a cool company or organization from outside your industry. Steal best practices from it.

DO THIS:

Step 1:

Generate a list of cool companies and organizations you admire—none of which should be direct or indirect competitors of your organization, or even in your own industry. Only add names to the list if you can provide substantive answers to the following questions about them:

- *What makes this organization different?*
- *What makes this organization cool?*
- *What makes this organization successful?*
- *What do I love about this organization?*
- *Is this organization a rule-breaker?*
- *Is this organization a rule-maker?*

Step 2:

As people are answering the above questions, put stars next to answers that generate group excitement. Discuss which of the starred qualities should be the highest priority for identifying an alien resource you want to study in depth. Pick something that makes you at least a little bit uncomfortable.

Step 3:

As a team (your Innovation Coalition), physically visit the organization you have selected, if possible. Study what that organization does exceptionally well.

Step 4:

Take an idea you've picked up from your alien influence—the bigger the better—and then set up and implement a plan for its execution within your own organization. (Yes, there can be more than one, but prioritize and attack each in order.)

GET THE "STEALING GENIUS FIELD GUIDE" PLUS MORE USEFUL INFORMATION AND TIPS! GO TO:

stealinggenius.com/resources

NOTES

1. I don't like calling them fans or followers. They're my friends.

2. I am simplifying, for the purposes of clarity, the American Girl product line, which is massive, but it is worth noting in passing that one of the offshoots of the classic, historically driven line of dolls is an online tool enabling girls to design their own American Girl dolls. The market for custom

dolls that resemble their young owners is apparently a robust one. This variant, too, is driven by strong emotional engagement: girls can (and do) create their own life stories with these dolls.

3. See Laura Rutherford-Morrison, "5 Ways American Girls Are Better Than Barbie," *Bustle*, January 6, 2015, https://www.bustle.com/articles/56685-5-ways-american-girl -dolls-are-so-much-better-than-barbie-for-young-girls.

Ideas for Stealing Genius

CH 4

STEALING GENIUS LEVEL 3: IDENTIFY A ROLE MODEL AND ASK YOURSELF, "WHAT WOULD THIS PERSON DO?"

"It's not where you take things from—it's where you take them to."

—Jean-Luc Godard

The third level of Stealing Genius is to think of a specific person from outside your industry or area of specialty and ask yourself, "What would that person do if they were faced with this same challenge I am facing?"

Note that at this level, the assumption is you *do* have a specific challenge to address or problem to solve. The person whose example you take into consideration can be living or dead. Of course, you will want to make sure you know enough about the person to formulate an accurate answer to this question.

WALKING THE TALK

Early on in the days of my consulting, I realized I had an important issue to address: I was not being congruent.

Here I was, helping business owners set up branding campaigns that allowed them to stand out from their competition—and yet my own company's messaging was inconsistent and not particularly compelling. We weren't sending a unified message. There came a point where I could no longer ignore that I needed to create a branding proposition that was organized around a single, powerful, and memorable promise. After all, that's what I was telling my clients to do. If I was going to be taken seriously, I had to set the example. I needed to walk my talk.

The big question was, whose example would *I* follow?

I kicked around various possibilities. There were the obvious ones—Walt Disney, Steve Jobs, Steven Spielberg, Albert Einstein, Pablo Picasso—and not so obvious—Agatha Christie, Stan Freberg, Ernie Kovacs, Saul Bass, Mary Kay Ash…

Mary Kay Ash!

I kept coming back to Mary Kay Ash, the late founder of the iconic Mary Kay Cosmetics firm.

Why did she keep popping up in my mind? How did Mary Kay Ash stand out from the competition? What would she do in this situation? I called to mind some famous stories, did a little research, and found the answer to that question pointed me toward two words that ended up transforming my organization and many of my clients' businesses: *anchors* and *triggers.*

In a stroke of inspiration that turned out to be one of the greatest branding maneuvers of all time, Mary Kay Ash opted, in 1963, to identify her organization with a single color—pink—and to make that color an *anchor* that laid the groundwork for greater awareness of her brand. So let's take a moment to consider exactly how that anchoring worked.

Pink was inescapable and ubiquitous in Mary Kay Ash's world; it defined her very first product, the Basic Treatment Set, and it was subsequently built into every imaginable touchpoint with the Mary Kay Cosmetics brand, both internal and external. Ash was totally committed to this plan, to a point some people might say bordered on obsession. Maybe it was, but the obsession came to define both her and her company.

Ash built her entire product packaging plan around the color pink. She designed all of her marketing materials around the color pink. She designed company stationery and envelopes around the color pink. She drove a pink Cadillac. Perhaps most famously, she leased pink Cadillacs to the "beauty consultants" (also known as salespeople) who managed to hit the coveted $100,000-a-year-in-sales level selling her cosmetics. The color pink in general, and specifically the iconic pink Cadillac, became, by design, strongly identified with her brand. Why? Because if you had any kind of interaction, at any point, for any length of time, with Mary Kay Ash's company, you connected that interaction, consciously or subconsciously, to the color pink.

All of that happened by design. Each of those pink touchpoints had a purpose: to create a bond in the observer's mind. Once that bond was established, the anchor was laid. All that had to happen next was for the observer to encounter a trigger.

Let's say you were that observer. Once you saw that color pink in any setting, from any source, for any reason—let's say, on a woman's dress—you would be more likely to start thinking about…you guessed it…Mary Kay Ash Cosmetics.

Did it work?

Let me answer that question by posing another: When I tell you Mary Kay Ash lived in a sprawling 30-room mansion that happened to be, you guessed it, pink, does that make you at all curious about the potential upside of a technique like this?[1] About what you might be able to achieve in terms of generating *top-of-mind* awareness…by deploying this *back-of-mind* branding approach? About what color you should claim for yourself and your operation?

By the way, I was once keynoting at a conference at the Dallas Anatole Hotel, a massive 1,606-room complex. Because of its size and design, the Anatole often held multiple big events at the same time. It just so happened Mary Kay was holding their annual convention at the same time I was speaking for the other event!

I was certainly curious, so I walked over to the side of the complex where Mary Kay's events were being held. To say I entered an alien experience is a true understatement. Hundreds of well-dressed and well-made-up (is that a word?) women filled the hotel lobby and hallways. Almost all were wearing the prerequisite Mary Kay pink in some fashion, mostly blazers festooned with huge recognition ribbons. Some had so many ribbons that they had pink lined all down their sleeves, as well!

The thing was…I was suddenly in a sea of PINK. If I'd been allergic to the color pink, I'd have been dead ten feet in. These women weren't just loyal clients. They were totally ATTACHED to Mary Kay!

That's the kind of attachment I wanted to create. I decided our business, like Mary Kay's, was going to have a signature color—and that the color would dominate *everything* I sent out from our firm that might conceivably touch the outside world. How would I select that color? And which color was most likely to attract interest—and action? I decided to make the process by which I got the answers to those questions a family affair.

I cut out a bunch of colors, laid them out on the floor, and asked my then-two-year-old daughter Kelly to pick one. She chose orange. A couple of days later, I repeated the experiment to see if the results would be the same. Kelly once again chose orange. That settled it for me. If my two-year-old daughter was drawn to the color orange so consistently, it must have *something* going for it. Orange officially became our company color. And it has been the company color for nearly three decades.

Before I asked myself how Mary Kay Ash would have approached this situation, we had five different, competing colors in five different configurations, depending on whether you were looking at a business card, an advertisement, a brochure, an envelope, or a sheet of stationery. This mishmash of colors didn't represent anything to our "moose." Now we are all about orange. From the moment Kelly chose orange the second time around, I knew there could be only one color for us. So now, whenever I hand out a business card, it's orange. Whenever we mail a letter, it's on letterhead dominated by one color—orange—and it comes in a matching envelope that is similarly dominated by one color: orange. Whenever I show up for a meeting that's close enough for me to drive to, I'm driving an orange Jeep. When I get out of that car, I'm wearing something orange. Take a look at the cover of my first book, *Uncopyable*, and you'll see that it is (all together now) orange! This book cover is, too!

And orange now stands for something. It's the anchor and trigger for our branding proposition, our promise to the marketplace. We want you to equate orange with UNCOPYABLE and subsequently with Steve Miller. We want it embedded in our moose's brains so deeply that whenever they see the color orange, they can't help but think—UNCOPYABLE...STEVE MILLER.

Let me tell you a true story about the extraordinary power of anchoring and triggering—and the power of following the example of a great role model like Mary Kay Ash. There's a gentleman in Houston, Texas, by the name of Jim McIngvale, also known as "Mattress Mack." He's quite a prominent figure in the state of Texas, not just for owning a chain of successful furniture stores and a popular radio station, but also for his commitment to the community. During Hurricane Harvey in 2017, Tropical Storm Imelda in 2019, and the 2021 Texas power crisis, McIngvale allowed displaced Texans to shelter from the cold by spending the night at his Gallery Furniture stores. He got a lot of positive public attention for that—all of it earned. Jim McIngvale is, as the popular phrase has it, "good people."

Here's why I mention him. I admired McIngvale. I wanted to start a conversation with him. I'd never talked with him before, so I sent him a copy of my book *Uncopyable*, the cover of which is, as I have mentioned, orange. As was the letterhead that accompanied the book. As was the envelope the book came in. And business card. And bookmark.

A few months later, I got a call from McIngvale. He explained what had motivated him to call me: He'd been at the Opening Day game for the Houston Astros baseball team the night before, and when he saw the Astros run out onto the field in the top of the first inning, he saw the orange color that dominates their jerseys. That reminded him of the orange book I had mailed him…and reminded him that he had meant to call me to talk about working together! He hired me for a two-day consulting assignment on the spot.

Anchor…trigger…engagement!

And no, I am not kidding when I tell you I owe that business, and much other business, to my chosen role model: Mary Kay Ash.

THE POSSIBILITIES ARE ENDLESS

Once you pick your role model, the sky really is the limit. You can generate some amazing breakthroughs—as long as that person *is not directly connected* to the industry or field in which you are operating. I'll share a couple of my favorite examples.

Another client of mine, Delphi Automotive, selected Steve Jobs as their role model. Their big question was: How could they stand out from other vendors at a crowded automotive aftermarket trade show? Answer: Model their booth after the Apple Genius Bar! That's what they did, creating a stunning combination of sleek showroom and high-octane problem-solving center. The response from participants at the show was overwhelmingly positive; the sales leads the booth generated were evidence enough of that.

WHO IS YOUR ROLE MODEL?

Let me share one more cool example of Stealing Genius Level 3 in action. Years ago, my brother, Scott, and I volunteered to coach a local Little League team for eight- to ten-year-olds. Frankly, our team wasn't very good.

Despite losing most of our games, we wanted the kids and their families to have a great time, and we knew the best way to do that was to ensure lots of loving faces showed up in the stands. So we asked ourselves: *Who is our role model? Who is really, really good at getting people to show up at ball games?*

We came up with two answers: Bill Veeck, the legendary baseball franchise owner and promoter par excellence, and his son Mike, who followed in his dad's footsteps as both an entrepreneur and a showman. We asked ourselves: *What would these guys do?* And the answer we came up with was: *Themed promotions for our games.*

If you've ever attended Major League Baseball games, you know what kind of promotions I mean. Both Veecks were famous for staging memorable, attention-grabbing events that got fans talking and brought them out to see baseball games—often, games played by home teams with losing records. For instance: The elder Veeck gave away live animals during games, held weddings at home plate, and hosted Grandstand Managers Night, in which fans used signs to vote on strategy decisions usually reserved for the manager! When you're looking for ways to get people to pay to see a last-place team, these are the kinds of things you come up with. The Veecks are definitely heroes of mine.

So we asked ourselves: *What sort of themed promotion would the Veecks do?* We studied their long and well-documented list of promotional ideas, including the now-legendary day they sent three-foot-seven-inch Eddie Gaedel up to the plate as a pinch hitter. Ultimately, we settled on a series of less sensational themed promotions, including Bat Night (on which we gave out miniature bats) and Photo Day (when we hired a photographer and invited families to stop by and have their picture taken with their favorite player). Our team and their families had a blast!

Good thing, too. We went 0-12. The players said that was because of the quality of the managerial decisions. We agreed to disagree on that one.

THE BIG TAKEAWAY:

Pick a role model. Ask yourself, *What would that person do?*

DO THIS:

Think of a specific person from outside your industry or area of specialty—someone you admire for one reason or another—and answer the following questions:

- 💡 *How did that person stand out from the competition?*
- 💡 *What would he or she do if faced with the same challenge I am facing?*
- 💡 Go big. Ask: *If he or she took over our organization, what would they do differently?*

GET THE "STEALING GENIUS FIELD GUIDE" PLUS MORE USEFUL INFORMATION AND TIPS! GO TO:

stealinggenius.com/resources

NOTE

1. The mansion itself was, of course, yet another anchor, one that Ash laid masterfully by generating ongoing media interest in her one-of-a-kind dwelling.

Ideas for Stealing Genius

STEALING GENIUS LEVEL 4: FLIP THE COMPETITION

"Invert, always invert."
—Carl Jacobi

The fourth level of Stealing Genius is to think of something a direct competitor of yours would do—and then find a way to do the polar opposite. Or, as I like to tell my clients, "Look at what everybody else is doing…and don't do it."

You may or may not have a specific business or team challenge to address at this level. In many cases, you will be looking at what has been accepted as orthodoxy by the major players in your field—and then looking for ways to turn that orthodoxy on its head.

What most organizations do is the inverse of this technique—and the opposite of innovation. They take a close look at their direct competitors and try to find ways to *keep up with* them or *improve on* them. This unfortunate choice leads, as we have seen, to an ever-accelerating spiral of commoditization and to ever-deepening vulnerability within your chosen field. Here, though, we are talking about something very different: taking a close look at our direct competitors (or our indirect competitors, for that matter) and looking for ways we can shake things up, and set ourselves apart, by taking an approach that is as different from theirs as we can possibly make it.

The technique I will be sharing with you in this chapter has been the wellspring of some truly great ideas. One of the most memorable comes from a rock-and-roll guitarist who also happened to be a business visionary.

JERRY GARCIA, INNOVATOR

> ## "I don't want to be the best in the world at what I do; I want to be the *only* one in the world who does what I do."
> ## —Jerry Garcia

The gist of the quote above, from legendary Grateful Dead co-founder Jerry Garcia, appears in countless different forms and shows up in a wide variety of sources. So I'm thinking he said this a lot. I'm sharing the version of the quote that seems most on target to me because it most directly relates to one of the major themes of this book, which is: *Don't just think outside the box—build a whole new box.*

The remarkable band Garcia led for three decades certainly built their own box musically. They also built their own box in terms of business strategy. How? By taking a good, long look at current trends in the music industry…and then exploring what would happen if they turned those ideas upside down. And by the way, if you doubt for one minute the Grateful Dead was, and is, a business, consider that, according to *Variety,* the band grossed, from licensing, royalties, live concerts with a Garcia-less lineup, and all other sources, well over $250 million between 2016 and 2020.

How did they get to that point? By inversion.

Inversion, reversal, or "thinking backwards"—all these labels are popular ways of describing what happens in the fourth level of Stealing Genius. Inversion is a classic creativity technique for artists. An example would be the street artist who leaves a design on a wall, not by applying paint, but by removing a layer of dirt to create a whole new image. This idea launched a major trend in urban art that has shown up in a number of cities. It's easy enough to see how it got started. You're an artist; you start looking at what someone else in your area of interest is doing (spraying stuff onto a wall), and then you start asking yourself, *What would happen if I were to find a way to do the opposite (removing material from a wall)?* That's inversion.

There are far too many examples of the Grateful Dead zagging when the rest of the music industry was zigging to list definitively in this or any other book…but I want to use this chapter to focus on the most revolutionary and influential choice Garcia and his bandmates made in alignment with this technique.

Garcia and his bandmates proved this way of thinking can be a potent innovation tool, not just on the artistic level, but on the organizational level, as well. They faced a classic challenge, one millions of business and team leaders can identify with: *How do we make this operation more profitable?* The Grateful Dead addressed that challenge by consistently asking themselves questions like:

What do most rock bands do to make money?

What if we were to do the opposite?

How is our audience different from the typical rock band's audience?

Questions like these can be liberating! When the Dead posed them, what they realized was *most* rock bands relied on record sales for their income. For most bands, generating royalties from the sale of their recordings was the whole point of going on tour: the concerts promoted album sales. Historically, the Dead hadn't sold in high volume, so they asked: *What if we did it the other way around? What if the records served as promotional vehicles for people to come to our concerts? What if concerts were the primary generator of the band's revenue?*

These were pretty daring questions to ask, but the Dead was a pretty daring band. They contemplated an entirely new business model, one that was predicated on their ability to continue drawing in concertgoers who would pay to see the band play not once, not twice, not three times, but *dozens* of times—at dozens of different venues. Absurd, right? Expecting people to follow the band around the country seems like the longest of longshots. Yet the Dead nurtured and supported that business model in collaboration with their extraordinarily loyal fan base. It was an idea no other band would be able to implement successfully for several decades, yet the Dead put it into practice by making an unparalleled strategic choice, one that was diametrically opposed to the strategy employed by most bands of that era. That choice had to do with what is now known as "taper culture."

To understand what "taper culture" is and how the Dead leveraged it to build deeper and deeper levels of loyalty and engagement within their remarkable base of repeat concertgoers, it helps to understand the band's backstory. In the late 1960s and early 1970s, the Dead was best understood as an ongoing countercultural experiment, one firmly rooted in the "free-everything" ethos of the Haight-Ashbury era in San Francisco. As the intense devotion of their fans became more and more impossible to ignore, with people following the band around the country to experience—and record—dozens or even hundreds of Dead shows, the band became known for turning a blind eye to fans who brought recording equipment to their concerts and taped their shows for their own private libraries. These people were, technically, violating copyright laws by taping, copying, and sharing homemade versions of Dead performances. Record company executives might have (and surely did) point out this sort of laissez-faire attitude was regarded as a threat to record sales. Yet the Dead realized encouraging exactly that kind of sharing was an extremely important promotional strategy.

In fact, since the mid-1980s, the Dead made it official policy to actively *support* the tapers by giving them a special section of their own, right behind the band's soundboard. The Dead weren't trying to maximize record sales. They were trying to maximize concert attendance. They had flipped the model. They wanted to support and deepen the concert experience and give people reasons to want to repeat it.

Enjoying great live music, of course, was a prime motivator, but the Dead knew the experience didn't start or stop there for their fans. Trading tapes of earlier concerts, it turned out, was a huge reason some people showed up at more than one Grateful Dead concert. (Back in the early 1970s, of course, that trading had to be done in person.). Connecting and socializing with other Dead fans was another important part of the decision to see multiple Dead shows. And feeling like you were part of a special tribe, members of a unique group that came into being only before, during, and right after Dead shows, was another reason people paid to see the Dead over and over again.

Based on what they heard and saw from fans, the band members built and continually refined a brand-new business model, one that did not rely on checks from record companies. This model flipped the orthodoxy. It was built around the idea that someone who was willing to pile into a van and drive hundreds of miles to hear the band play for the tenth, fiftieth, or hundredth time would encourage others to do the same—if that meant they could rejoice, repeatedly, in a shared identity: being part of the emerging "tribe" known as Deadheads.

That was the name adopted by the distinctive community the band decided to support. The endlessly adaptive, endlessly loyal community of Deadheads constituted, not so much a classic fan club of a rock and roll band, as a mobile village committed to a certain way of life they saw the Dead as embodying. The band's music lay at the heart of the lifestyle they were willing to travel for, sacrifice for, contribute to in ways large and small, build their social calendar around—and yes, buy tickets for.

Garcia and company's decision to serve that community by means of a special kind of concert experience made them the antithesis of the traditional rock band. Most bands, for instance, played the same set list in every city. The Grateful Dead didn't. *Most* bands, *most* promoters, *most* concert security details treated people who came to rock and roll concerts like wayward teens, potential problems, troublemakers-in-waiting. They treated paying customers like kids who needed harsh rules imposed on them in order to keep disaster from playing out before, during, and after the concert. The Grateful Dead didn't. And of course, they knew *most* rock bands strictly forbade recording equipment at concerts. The Grateful Dead didn't do that, either. Instead, they made it a central part of the Grateful Dead subculture.

The band supported that subculture in countless other ways, including allowing fans to set up stands to sell their wares to other Deadheads. And they have continued to support that subculture long after the Grateful Dead yielded, with Garcia's passing, to the band known as Dead & Company. And it all began with the choice to treat Deadheads with audio recording equipment like what they manifestly were, and what they still are today: part of a family. They transformed the concert experience from something designed to move people in and out of a venue quickly…to something very different: a mobile city, a huge traveling flea market rooted in communal values and driven by an ever-varying musical heartbeat of Grateful Dead songs.

Through inversion, the Grateful Dead created a breakthrough revenue model that flipped the orthodoxy. It did that by breaking new ground by delivering and refining what I like to call a *richly imprinted experience*, meaning an experience that wants to be imprinted, remembered, and shared. In so doing, they planted the seeds for the astonishing, exponential growth of their brand over the years.

If you want to see what all the fuss is about and share first-hand in the ongoing Deadhead experience, you can. That experience has been evolving for over half a century now. The successor band Dead & Company (featuring legacy band members Bob Weir, Mickey Hart, and Bill Kreutzmann) is still going strong, and yes, you can even download publicly shared digital recordings of their concerts by visiting the website livedead.co. Check it out. I predict you'll be glad you did. Whether you experience them live or via the latest expression of the taper-culture legacy, you will find them to be a band like no other.

TURN THE PARADIGM UPSIDE DOWN

Examples abound of companies flipping the competition.

- When the big airlines adopted the hub-and-spoke strategy, Southwest Airlines countered with point-to-point.

- When computer manufacturers were turning out bland lookalikes, Steve Jobs went the opposite direction, making design and CX (customer experience) a critical strategic advantage for Apple.

- Tesla doesn't have dealerships. They have stores and galleries, mostly in large shopping malls.

- Uber flipped the taxi industry completely on its head. In most cities, you must purchase an expensive medallion that gives you the right to drive a taxi. Uber gives you the ability to earn money with your own car.

- Similar to the Uber model, Airbnb revolutionized short-term home-sharing between users online.

Sit down with your Innovation Coalition and start a list of common behaviors, unwritten rules, and business models your competitors (and probably you) follow. Especially look for those that directly impact your customer.

For example, I told you in a previous chapter about Mattress Mack (Jim McIngvale), the Texas-based home furnishing entrepreneur and impresario who called me after spotting the color orange at a Houston Astros baseball game.

While I was in Houston working with him and his team at Gallery Furniture, he asked me to sit in on a meeting with his warehouse and delivery staff. I found out Jim had implemented a beautiful flip on his competition with deliveries.

I think I can safely say the majority of home furnishing companies think of deliveries from an "efficiency" perspective. In other words, if I purchase a new couch, the delivery people will show up, bring the couch inside, have me sign for the delivery, and be on their way to the next delivery. Efficiency is the goal. That's the common approach.

Not for Jim McIngvale. Jim correctly understood the importance of the delivery experience. It is the last impression and touchpoint the customer has from the purchase. He looked for a way to make that last impression not just okay or even just good. He wanted to make it amazing.

Jim gave his delivery people instructions to ask the following question before leaving the customer's property:

What else do you need done around your home that we can help you with?

When the delivery guy posed this question to a customer who owned a farm, the customer responded that her husband was ill and unable to exercise the horses and milk the cows. Could Mattress Mack's delivery team help with that?

Without blinking an eye, they assured her they could. It turned out both had grown up on farms. One took care of the cattle, and the other exercised the horses.

What kind of an impact do you think that made on the customer? Do you think she'll buy from Gallery Furniture again? Do you think she told anyone about this experience?

By flipping the common approach to deliveries, Jim McIngvale is creating attachment…a lifetime customer.

Not long ago, I mentioned this story in a webinar I was conducting, and one participant said, "I would never tell my delivery people to do anything like that. Their job is to get back on the road to the next delivery!"

I replied: "Then you'd better hope Mattress Mack isn't your competition!"

THE BIG TAKEAWAY:

Look at what everyone else in your industry is doing—and then do the opposite.

DO THIS:

Sit down with your Innovation Coalition and create a list of common behaviors, unwritten rules, and business models your competitors (and probably you) follow. Especially look for those that directly impact your customer.

Then identify a way to shake things up by taking an approach that is as different to theirs as you can possibly make it. For example, if your competition answers the phone in person, how can you flip it to NOT answer the phone in person, yet design it in a way to be a competitive advantage?

GET THE "STEALING GENIUS FIELD GUIDE" PLUS MORE USEFUL INFORMATION AND TIPS! GO TO:

stealinggenius.com/resources

Ideas for Stealing Genius

CH 6

STEALING GENIUS LEVEL 5: KEEP YOUR RADAR UP 24/7

"Let us not look back in anger, nor forward in fear, but around in awareness."

—James Thurber

The fifth level of Stealing Genius is to be open to influences from any source, at any time, that can point you toward genius you can steal.

I'll be frank with you: this level takes time and dedication to understand and practice. It's the black belt of Stealing Genius.

We all bring preconceptions to our day, and we are all subject to the all-too-human tendency to rely on our own skill set, our own assumptions, our own history, when it comes to dealing with challenges. We are all hardwired to stay within our comfort zone and see things from our own perspective. We can't help it. (We'll be looking at why this is so in chapter 8.)

My point is, this technique is the exact opposite of what you are used to doing. It is an ongoing commitment to leave yourself open to *any* influence, *any* inspiration, *any* insight that comes from a place that lies beyond your "box"—your current area of expertise. Making this standard operating procedure will not happen overnight. Earning a black belt in a martial arts discipline does not happen overnight either. But if you get started and if you are persistent, you will be closer to black-belt-level mastery today than you were yesterday.

THE TWO BIG QUESTIONS, REVISITED

Do you remember the story I told you about de Mestral at the beginning of this book, about how he saw something interesting in the way burrs got stuck in his clothing after he had walked his dog? Do you remember the two questions that pointed him toward the breakthrough he needed to Steal Genius and create Velcro?

Just in case you don't, here they are again:

What is really happening here?

Where else could this be used?

These questions are the mantra of a Stealing Genius Black Belt. We are talking about the art of noticing what is right in front of you, no matter how unremarkable or far removed from your world it might seem at first…and then asking yourself how that might connect to a challenge or problem you are facing. From one perspective, this is the work of a lifetime. From another, it is something you can easily implement in any waking moment, including this one, because (as de Mestral's story proves) there is possibility in every moment of our lives. Entering the fifth level of Stealing Genius simply means being present 24/7 to the possibility there is some new example of genius you can steal standing right in front of you. You just don't know where or when you're going to find it.

A LESSON FROM A LOWBROW DINER

Let me give you an example of what I am talking about. I will sometimes hold multi-day in-person sessions for clients from multiple (noncompetitive) companies. Some people call these sessions "boot camps," but I prefer to call them "laboratories," because for me the emphasis is less on discipline than on learning how to discover…to see with new eyes—and discovery is what happens in a laboratory.

On the first morning of a recent event, I set up a big Stealing Genius surprise—an unexpected lesson for all the participants. I took them all out for breakfast at a distinctly informal establishment in Downtown Seattle called The 5 Point Cafe. What, you may ask, does taking a group of executives out to breakfast at a distinctly lowbrow Seattle diner have to do with the fifth Stealing Genius level? Everything. When is a diner not a diner? Read on.

When we got back to the conference room where I was conducting the program, I asked, "What did you think of that diner where we just had breakfast? Tell me about your impressions. What did you think about the entire experience of going to The 5 Point Cafe? Was it a positive for you? A negative? Were you neutral about it? What did you notice?"

The participants told me they didn't really have a very positive impression of the place, that they were surprised I had taken them someplace like that. This was what I had expected.

I asked, "Did any of you happen to study the menu closely enough to get a glimpse of the restaurant's motto?"

Nobody had. I said, "Would it surprise you to learn that for many years, the place where we just had breakfast was voted the No. 1 dive bar in the city of Seattle?"

I was met with puzzled looks. They hadn't even been aware there was competition to *become* the No. 1 dive bar in the city of Seattle. I love Seattle.

I said, "None of you realized it, but our two-day laboratory started at The 5 Point Cafe. What can you tell me about the kind of customer this place targets—and how do you know that? What can you tell me about its organizational culture? And again, how do you know? There were some very clear signals sent."

Crickets. No one in the conference room had expected there to be questions like these about the unassuming diner—let's face it, the *dive*—I had just taken them to. We went there for breakfast, and I hadn't given them any instructions. They all looked at me, confused and uncertain about what, exactly, they should have been taking notes on. I let the silence linger for a while. Then I pulled out The 5 Point Cafe menu (I had a copy of my own just for moments like this. Yes, I stole it. I think The 5 Point Cafe would be proud.) I asked one of the participants to read aloud the line that appeared at the very bottom of that menu. We all heard him say:

The Five Point Cafe: Alcoholics serving alcoholics since 1929.

I asked: "How much does that one sentence tell you?"

There followed a vigorous discussion of everything The 5 Point Cafe had managed to convey with that extraordinary (and, for the participants in my program, entirely unseen) tagline. For instance:

- **This sentence tells you *exactly* who The 5 Point Cafe targets as its primary customer.** (In other words, they know their moose!) Clearly, it's tongue-in-cheek, but even the language is carefully constructed to appeal unapologetically to their moose.

- There were plenty of other signals about this, all of which went unnoticed by the participants in my program. For instance: signs announcing The 5 Point Cafe's expansive "happy hour" policy—6:00 to 9:00 a.m. and 4:00 to 6:00 p.m. That's two "happy hours" for the price of one, if you're keeping score at home. Then there are the various unforgettable signs that greet patrons who enter the joint. One of my favorites: "We cheat tourists and drunks." There were quite a few more signs with very raw messages. Translation: This is a dive bar that refuses to apologize for being a dive bar, one that also happens to serve very good food. It targets people who want to drink alcohol and who, like the restaurant, refuse to apologize for their choices. They are very supportive of everybody. If you are LGBTQ+, this is a safe place. You must treat everyone well if you want to spend time here. The menu also included this warning to patrons:

WARNING: The 5 Point welcomes all types of people, including those in various states of inebriation, and with sometimes extremely different political, religious, and social ideologies. We pour stiff drinks, play loud music, and serve large portions of the best diner food in Seattle, in a very casual atmosphere with a no-nonsense, irreverent attitude. If you are easily offended, there's a good chance you will be offended here. Our loyal regulars have always loved our no-nonsense approach to customer service, and that's why we have the best clientele anywhere in Seattle. We are sorry if you are offended by the foul mouthed security guys or rowdy strippers (or nurses, roofers, or off work restaurant staff, etc.) sitting at the table next to you, or if you think the music is too loud. But these are our people, and we love them. So love them too, or leave.

- **This sentence also tells you whom the restaurant *does not* target.** If you have recently enrolled in a 12-step program, this is probably not the place for you to book a table for brunch (or work, for that matter). Nor is it a family restaurant. If you are, for whatever reason, eager to stay sober, or looking for somewhere fun to take the kids, the message from The 5 Point Cafe is clear: go somewhere else.

- **This sentence also tells you exactly who this company is and what it stands for.** At The 5 Point Cafe, they've figured that out…and they are happy to talk about it with any and all comers. This is a critical component of establishing and living a clearly defined workplace culture: being able to communicate it. Once you can communicate it, you can live it. If you can't communicate it, you can't expect to live it consistently, and you can't expect anyone else to live it, either.

Someone in the group asked, "How does learning The 5 Point culture help us?"

"By helping you learn to *notice where you are 24/7, even if it's a place like The 5 Point Cafe,* so you can decide for yourself whether there is anything you want to steal from them. My point is, nobody in this room even picked up on that statement: *The 5 Point Cafe: Alcoholics serving alcoholics since 1929.* That's culture. That's powerful branding. That's recruiting. That's everything! So I want you to start noticing things like that everywhere you go. You can't decide whether you want to steal something until you notice it first! My goal for all of you is to make it second nature for you to examine *every* experience you encounter, *every* interaction you take part in, and be able to ask yourself whether there's any genius at work you can steal on behalf of your own team or organization. I want you to notice the success stories. I want you to notice the failures. I want you to constantly check the radar screen to see if there's anything coming at you that you can commandeer and make your own. If they know their moose, do you know your moose just as well? How is their moose different from your moose? Or are there overlaps? If they communicate their culture clearly and coherently, do you communicate yours just as clearly and just as coherently? Is your culture the same as theirs or is it very different? Regardless, do you walk your talk as well as they walk theirs? Or better? I want you to constantly have your radar up, and I want you to constantly be thinking, *What are they doing and what can I steal?"*

What I was doing was prompting them to be aware for what I call "24/7 moments." As the name suggests, these can happen at any time of the day or night. So even when you're going out to breakfast, you're not *just* going out to breakfast. Even when you go to a Starbucks, you're not just going to get coffee. Even when you check into a hotel, you're not just getting a room. You're always open to what you can learn, what you can adapt, what new connections you can make that might be able to bring you to the threshold of a breakthrough.

When you can consistently achieve that level of automatic awareness, you become a Stealing Genius Black Belt, and the ideas will absolutely avalanche down on you. You might even have trouble writing them all down!

MAKE THE CONNECTIONS, EVEN WHEN YOU'RE OFF THE CLOCK

Very often, I'll do work with clients who are looking for ways to better identify their target markets. Recently, I had a "24/7 moment" that pointed me toward an idea in this area I could share with them. It would never have happened if I hadn't been open to the possibility of Stealing Genius from an unexpected source at an unexpected time.

One evening, my wife Kay and I were watching Ken Burns's excellent documentary series on country music (which, by the way, I highly recommend). Technically, of course, we were engaged in a leisure activity as we were doing this. It was well after 5:00. But if I had had my Stealing Genius radar off just because I was in downtime mode, I never would have had my breakthrough. Sidenote: *It's an entirely positive, energizing experience to have a 24/7 moment when you're not "on the clock."* Why? Because your brain is open to new ideas and new possibilities, which means you're turning work into play—and vice versa! So don't shut down the possibility of innovation just because you're not in the office.

So anyway, there we were, watching the Ken Burns documentary, when we saw a fascinating detail that illustrated just how popular the Grand Ole Opry was back in the 1930s: you could drive through Southern towns and hear, through the open windows of the houses, the radio broadcast of the live Grand Ole Opry performance taking place that night. Here's the interesting part: A big insurance company, one of the sponsors of the broadcast, paid its salespeople to do just that—walk through towns and listen for the sound of that night's Grand Ole Opry broadcast. The salespeople would jot down the addresses of the houses with families who were listening to the show. The next day, the salesperson would show up at the house, knock on the door, and introduce himself. Did the family listen to the Grand Ole Opry? (Of course, the salesperson knew the answer was "Yes.") He would then pull a Grand Old Opry souvenir out of his bag and say, "My company is the sponsor for the Grand Old Opry, and since you listen to it, we'd like you to have this special gift. May I come in for a minute?" (That answer was almost always "Yes," too.)

A few minutes' discussion about the previous night's broadcast turned out to be a great rapport-builder and a far stronger conversation starter than "Can I talk to you about buying some insurance?" Long story short, a lot of those salespeople closed deals with new customers... because they were willing to identify a critical common factor that defined one group of prospective buyers: they were listening to the Grand Ole Opry broadcast sponsored by the insurance company. Just in case you're keeping score at home: listening to the Grand Ole Opry was another of those richly imprinted experiences I talked to you about earlier—an experience that wants to be remembered, shared, and repeated. *Of course,* people would invite a salesperson bearing gifts in for a chat!

This anecdote reminded my wife Kay of something she had seen while she was making a visit to one of her clients during her time as a salesperson. This was an auto repair shop. Kay noticed that when a customer dropped off a vehicle, one of the things the manager of the auto shop would do before starting work on the customer's car was to turn on the radio and take written note of which stations the car radio had preset as favorites. Kay asked the auto shop manager why he did that. He said, "We like to know what stations they listen to because that helps us to decide which station to buy advertising on." What a great idea! And it followed the same basic principle as the story in the country music documentary: identify a critical common factor that defines your prospective buyers. Find something that unifies them. Then use that something as a point of contact and engagement in the future.

> Let me take a little pirouette here (I HATE using the abused word *pivot*) and give you a recent example of being a Stealing Genius Black Belt that ties in with the radio station example. In this case, I spotted an example of a worst practice in the marketplace that still gave me an idea!

Not long ago, I had my new Jeep Cherokee in the dealership for some routine service. (Yes, my Jeep is ORANGE, and it's HOT.) When I dropped it off, I was listening to a sports talk station in Seattle. Apparently, this dealer doesn't practice what Kay's automotive repair shop practices. When I picked up my Jeep, the dial had been changed to a hip-hop station. I have nothing against hip-hop, but a) it's not what I listen to and b) having people switch around my radio stations is a little like having people root through my underwear drawer. Not cool. So yes, I noticed. And yes, it irritated me. It's never the lions and tigers that get you in the jungle. It's the mosquitoes!

Just now, as I was writing about Kay's customer, I connected with my own experience. Let me share the thoughts running through my head:

The Jeep dealer is clearly not paying much attention to their moose. In fact, they're unleashing mosquitoes on them!

That creates opportunity for their competition. If Kay's client was one of those competitors, what could they do? Here are some ideas:

- Go beyond just paying attention to what station their customer listens to.

- When the customer picks up their car, leave a nice note on the dash with something like, "Thank you once again for allowing ABC Auto to service your vehicle! We noticed you had your radio dial tuned into KJR-AM. Did you know we advertise on that station? We want to acknowledge our customer Rock Stars, like you, by giving away a free front-end alignment! Keep listening to KJR. If you hear one of our commercials mention your name and you call us within 60 minutes, you'll win that alignment. And to help increase your odds, please tell your friends to listen to KJR for your name. If they hear it and let you know and you call in, you'll BOTH win front-end alignments! GOOD LUCK!"

That's 24/7 Stealing Genius Awareness. And now, back to our regularly scheduled program.

Back to the Grand Ole Opry. What connects the Grand Ole Opry story with the story about Kay's customer, the auto repair shop? A powerful idea: Figure out something the people you want to communicate and engage with have in common. Don't just talk to *any and every* family on the block. Start with the ones you know you can have a better conversation with, the ones who have already had some kind of exposure to your brand and are likely to be positively disposed toward it. And don't just advertise on *any* radio station. Figure out which stations your customers are most likely to listen to…get a large enough sample size… and meet them where they already are!

I've shared these two stories with lots of my own clients, and they've helped get them to apply the same principle in their own efforts to engage with the highest-value contacts and potential sales leads: *find something your best customers have in common, and work from there.* Ask yourself: *Where do my customers and my best prospects hang out?*

If I had had my radar down, if I had not been open to the possibility of identifying unexpected sources of genius I could steal, I never would have been able to pass this principle and this collection of true stories on to my clients…or to you!

ISAAC NEWTON KEEPS HIS RADAR UP

In a remarkable essay called "The Reach of Imagination," published shortly before the Apollo 11 moon landing, the great mathematician and historian Jacob Bronowski shared an example that, for me, illustrates how one of the great scientists in human history, Sir Isaac Newton, followed the guidance I'm sharing with you in this chapter.

The seventeenth century, the one in which Newton grew up, was chock-full of speculations about a topic that would have fallen within the genre called "science fiction," if that term had existed at the time. The subject in question was one that captured the imagination and the attention of the learned of the day: a human being making a trip to the moon.

Of course, in Newton's time, this was the purest kind of fantasy, but it was fantasy that carried with it a healthy serving of curiosity. The writer Francis Godwin, a great-uncle of Jonathan Swift's, published a fanciful story on this theme in 1638 entitled *The Man in the Moone,* and we know Isaac Newton was familiar with it. The historians are still squabbling about exactly when this book was written and whether it qualifies as the first science-fiction novel in human history. For our purposes, that debate is irrelevant. The point is, the book was popular for decades, and Newton read it as a young man. It got him thinking.

Inspired by (among other things) Godwin's fictional speculations, Newton sat in his mother's garden and started asking himself questions. What kinds of questions, exactly? We'll never know for certain, of course, but it's likely they sounded like these:

- What is gravity?

- What is its reach?

- How does it affect physical objects like the moon?

- What if the moon were like a ball thrown so hard that, under the influence of the Earth's gravitational pull, it fell just as fast as the horizon, all the way around the earth?

We can reconstruct such questions for a simple reason, a reason that staggers the imagination and serves as one of the great endorsements in human history for the practice of Stealing Genius from an unexpected source.

The unexpected source was Godwin's novel.

The reason we know questions like this must have occurred to Newton after he read that novel is when he was 23, Newton began attempting to calculate just how long the moon would take to circle the earth if it acted like that thrown ball that falls predictably and consistently in alignment with the horizon.

So what did the young mathematician find out when he crunched the numbers? He came up with an answer that was close enough to observed reality to inspire a course of scientific inquiry that would change everything. The young mathematician's handwritten figures told him the moon would complete such a circuit in 28 days.

Godwin's book had, through Isaac Newton, initiated a revolution in science.

So here is my question: Suppose the young Newton had *not* kept his radar up 24/7? Suppose he had dismissed storytelling as being irrelevant to mathematics and astronomy? Suppose he had seen Godwin's novel as a distraction from the serious business of rigorous scientific discovery? The history of humankind might have been very different.

Thank goodness, Newton was a Stealing Genius Black Belt.

THE BIG TAKEAWAY:

Never stop asking: What is really happening here? Where else could this be used?

DO THIS:

Reflect on three experiences you had today or yesterday—ideally, ones that do not connect directly with your organization. For each one, ask yourself whether there's any genius at work that you can steal on behalf of your own team or organization.

If you struggle to make any Stealing Genius connections from your recent experience, keep your antennae up going forward, mining every encounter for possible sources of innovation. And for today, perform the following exercise:

- The next time you're at a restaurant, a Starbucks, a mall, a retail store, take a moment to simply OBSERVE. Observe how they make their first impression. Observe how they greet people. Observe how they tell their story (do they have a story?). How do they attract your attention? Write down these observations.

- Later, review your notes and determine how you and/ or your organization compares with each item. Look for any differences, no matter how small or trivial.

- Ask the question, "Is there anything we should steal?"

GET THE "STEALING GENIUS FIELD GUIDE" PLUS MORE USEFUL INFORMATION AND TIPS! GO TO:

stealinggenius.com/resources

Ideas for Stealing Genius

CH 7

STEALING GENIUS LEVEL 6:
CHART AND CHOREOGRAPH THE
UNCOPYABLE EXPERIENCE

"People ignore design that ignores people."
—Frank Chimero

The sixth Stealing Genius level involves choreographing the Uncopyable experience. It's at this level that you put what you've learned in Levels 1 through 5 into practice.

Up to this point, we've looked at a lot of different perspectives on *what* you can do to Steal Genius. The purpose of this chapter is to show you *how* it might work in action.

This is a powerful tool that can really make a huge difference for you, not only from a marketing perspective, but in any area of your organization. It's one of the most important weapons in your arsenal when it comes to setting yourself apart from the competition—which is (we must always remember) something that has to happen both internally and externally. What I am about to share with you should be considered part of W. Edwards Deming's extrinsic benchmarking process, which is meant to be used in every corner of your organization.

No aspect of your operation should ever be considered finished! Every aspect can benefit from innovation.

The basic concept behind this tool is simple: *the totality of customer touchpoints impacts and creates the customer's ultimate experience.*

The totality of customer touchpoints impacts and creates the customer's ultimate experience.

Whenever a customer buys from you or works with you in any way, there are multiple, often many, touchpoints (impressions, interactions, and transactions that may or may not involve people) that customer navigates along the way.

Understand the customer's experience with you may start long before you actually have contact with them. For instance: visiting your website is a touchpoint. Receiving an email broadcast is a touchpoint. The way you answer the phone is a touchpoint. Whenever someone who *could* become a customer, or who could help someone else decide to become a customer, encounters any aspect of your organization—whether that's online, via videoconference, or in person while visiting your office, store, or factory, or any other facility—they, too, navigate multiple touchpoints. For instance: seeing your company's branded truck drive by while they're out on a walk. In each case, those touchpoints add up to and create an overall *experience* with your organization. And here's the point: you can design and manage the user experience.

Most of the time, organizations don't consciously bother to do that. They don't take the time or invest the attention and resources necessary to identify or choose all (or even some) of the touchpoints that add up to create an experience. They don't design the experience. In fact, too often, there isn't a lot of thought put into it at all. Typically, they just do what everyone else does. As a result, they end up offering a *low-quality* experience, one that is not memorable in any positive, influence-building way and doesn't set the organization apart from others in their industry.

By following the process I'm about to share with you, you're going to *design*—or as I prefer to call it, *choreograph*—that experience consciously and make it uniquely yours.

But before we choreograph the experience, we must first chart the existing touchpoints. Let's start by looking at the typical retail experience people might have in, say, a shopping mall. And then let's think about how we could innovate and transform that experience using the strategy shared in an earlier chapter: identifying a role model and asking ourselves what that person would do. (You could have used any of the other strategies, of course, but let's use that one for the sake of this example.) We'll assume the role model we will be looking at is Steve Jobs, the legendary co-founder of Apple. We'll ask ourselves: What would Jobs do?

TWO DIFFERENT PATHS

We are contrasting two paths. One path is the usual one, the one just about everyone else walks, the default experience, the path that feels familiar and common. The other path is the one rooted in innovation. You'll see they are very different paths. First let's examine the undesigned, or barely designed, experience. What does that first path look like in a retail setting?

Well, you walk into the mall, and you meander around for a bit. You find a store that interests you. You wander in and out of that store, and you wander in and out of various other stores. Truth be told, the mall journey is hard to separate from the store journey. The whole thing is fluid and a bit chaotic. Things overlap. The noise and bustle from the areas outside the store flow into whatever store you happen to be visiting, so that, for instance, if a child is crying or a couple of people happen to be arguing out in the walkway, you hear that clearly while you're exploring whatever store you've decided to visit. That store, by the way, has a cash register or two strategically located, so you can make your purchases and exit. Which is pretty much the whole idea.

The store considers you part of the "foot traffic" the mall is designed to generate; you're there to make a purchase, whether it's planned or unplanned. Basically, the store layout steers you toward the cash registers, which is, of course, the store's big touchpoint. The touchpoints that *precede* that decision to either buy something and pay for it at the cash register or leave the store and find another store to wander through include: signage (most of it announcing pricing), staff (typically disengaged and not well trained), the layout of the aisles, the shelving, mirrors, and the displays—none of which, truth be told, are all that radically different from the signage with pricing, disengaged staff, layout, shelving, and displays of most of the other stores in the mall. There are some differences from store to store, sure, but let's be honest—at the end of the day, you're not going to remember a whole bunch about any of those elements. You may remember things about products or decisions you made, of course, but the specific touchpoints you encounter along the way aren't likely to leave much of an impression on you. Then, of course, there's the combined effect of all the sounds and distractions from the rest of the mall. That's a touchpoint, too.

So, you wander in. Signage, pricing, disengaged staff, layout, shelving, displays, noise. You head to the cash register or you don't. You wander out. That's the typical, default, unremarkable experience offered by a retail outlet in a mall.

We've now charted a typical experience. Am I generalizing a little? Sure. Does that generalizing resonate even slightly with what you usually experience when you go to a mall? I'm thinking it might. Now, let's ask ourselves some Stealing Genius questions and see how we can choreograph this:

- *Which touchpoints do we have control over?*

- *Which touchpoints are we basically copying from our competition?*

- *Can we redesign any of those touchpoints as our own?*

- *How many touchpoints can we redesign to create an experience that allows us to stand out from the competition?*

- *What would Steve Jobs do?*

Questions like these lie at the heart of the *Choreographing the Uncopyable Experience* process, which is all about finding and following that second pathway. In this example, we're going to think like Steve Jobs. Let's look at the Apple Store and how they choreograph the Uncopyable experience.

HOW THE APPLE STORE CHOREOGRAPHS THE UNCOPYABLE EXPERIENCE

The Apple Store is a great example of a carefully designed, perfectly executed experience that instantly sets itself apart from other players. If you've ever been to an Apple Store, you know it's totally different than the experiences offered by other stores in the mall. And if you haven't visited an Apple Genius Bar in the back, I'm going to guess you've passed it and found yourself wondering about what was going on in there. You could see people talking to Apple employees who somehow seemed a little cooler and a little more knowledgeable than the typical cash register attendant, and you could see people picking up Apple products and, well, playing with them. Engaged customers! Taking their time! Exploring! And in no rush to leave!

So…how did Steve Jobs generate that experience?

By moving beyond what everyone else was doing. By designing a whole different set of touchpoints. On purpose! Let's look at just a few of those touchpoints now and notice how radically different they are from the touchpoints you encounter at the other stores in the mall.

Start at the front door.

Did you notice there was a front door to get into most Apple Stores? Did it occur to you how rare it is for a store inside the mall to have a front door? That didn't happen by accident. It's not just a design choice; it's a "choreograph the experience" choice. Opening a door means you are *choosing* to leave one space and enter another. It means you are crossing a threshold. It means you are taking up physical, mental, and emotional residence in a whole different location than you were before. That's what Apple wants to make sure happens before you step into their world. Which is what this is: a different world within the common world of the mall.

Every Apple Store has a prominent clear glass front.

Over the years, any number of unimaginative constituencies at malls and municipalities have tried—and failed—to get Apple's exterior to look like the exteriors of other stores. They've always lost. The glass front is a critical part of an Apple Store, and it's one of many elements that are congruent from Apple Store to Apple Store. That's not an accident, and it's not cheap! This is a deliberate choice, an essential element of the strategic plan that operates on two levels: First and foremost, it embodies Apple's values of creativity, adventure, and togetherness. You can see all of those things happening through that big glass window—which brings us to the second level. That's curiosity. When you pass the Apple Store, you inevitably *notice* that huge glass storefront, and you *see* those Apple users inside, chatting with those cool-looking Apple employees and playing with those cool-looking Apple toys...and you start wondering whether you ought to pay a visit yourself. How different is that from, say, the discount clothing store you just walked past? There is, however, an important touchpoint I suspect Jobs borrowed from another notable retailer, however, namely...

You're greeted at the door.

Walmart has a greeter who says "hello" to you as you enter the store; the Apple Store does, too. However, I would argue the Apple Store greeter has a different and more strategically vital role to play, a role whose importance would have been obvious to Jobs. Sure: Both the Walmart greeter and the Apple Store greeter establish one-on-one rapport with the visitor to the store; however, just about everyone knows what a Wal-Mart store is and how it works. Many people *don't* know how an Apple Store works, and a fair number of those people who don't know have never bought an Apple product before. The greeter puts newcomers at ease, identifies the reason for the visit, gives people their bearings, and helps them to figure out what they want to do next. That's essential in a technology setting, and it's particularly crucial for a company like Apple, which has made simplicity, user-friendliness, and ease of access part of their brand promise. The greeter points you in the right direction and, if you need help, connects you with someone who can help you. This touchpoint, too, was surely the result of end-user feedback from people who felt confused and irritated by "help lines" that weren't helpful and "service desks" that felt hard to access and get service from.

There are no posted prices and no cash registers.

Even though this is a retail outlet, there are no price tags connected to any of those Apple products. If you want to know how much one costs, just ask. If you want to buy something, one of the cool-looking Apple employees will pull out a card reader and help you to complete the transaction. I'd be willing to bet these touchpoints were designed, at least in part, as a result of feedback from end users who described feeling pressured to buy at other tech retailers. There is no pressure to purchase anything and no judgment on you if you opt not to. Clearly, Jobs wanted the polar opposite of the consumer experience people had come to expect at other stores.

Need customer service? Book an appointment.

All the other stores in the mall expect you to make your way through the aisles so you can eventually present yourself at the cash register to make a purchase (or try to sneak out unnoticed without doing so). But the Apple Store has a whole different dynamic. If you're there for something to do with a problem or question regarding your Apple product, you book an appointment online to talk to an Apple Genius in store. (Note the phrasing. They don't have "service technicians" or "customer service reps." Apple knows language matters.) While you wait, you can play with the new, cool Apple toys. And even if you're not there for a specific service or question, you can still *just* play with the cool Apple toys. That's fine, too.

I could go on, but I think I've listed enough touchpoints above to give you a sense of what this process looks like. Your goal is to create as many touchpoints as possible that set you apart from your competitors. If we were to make a list of the touchpoints that Jobs and company made a conscious choice to design and deploy in this way, it would contain all of the elements I've just mentioned:

- Front door/threshold experience (sets store apart from traffic, noise, etc.; critical early touchpoint)

- Glass storefront (no other store looks like that)

- Greeted at the door, pointed in right direction (human touch, based on user feedback)

- No cash registers; staff equipped with card readers (the human being is the touchpoint)

- No posted prices; staff answers questions about pricing or anything else (the human being is the touchpoint)

- Book an appointment—if you want (human touch, based on user feedback)

- Play with cool tech toys as long as you want; no pressure to buy (human touch, based on user feedback)

So let's say, for the sake of argument, we are trying to stand out by delivering a truly Uncopyable experience in the mall where we have a store...and let's also assume we don't compete with the Apple Store. Here's the big question: What could we steal from Steve Jobs's way of thinking? What could we adapt in our world that no one else in our mall is adapting?

- Could we set up a "threshold experience" like the experience of opening the door to the Apple Store? Could we find a way to create a whole new world, inside the world of the mall but distinct from it? No, we don't have to build an actual wall with an actual door...but could we find a way to make the point of entry into our store a conscious commitment? The fact is, there are other stores that do that: Tommy Bahama, Abercrombie & Fitch, Tiffany & Co., and Tumi, for example. Did you notice them?

- Could we create a "storefront" unlike anything else in the mall?

- Could we assign someone to greet people as they enter our store?

- Could we find other ways to leverage the human touch that other stores in our mall aren't able to?

- Could we take out the cash registers, equip our people with card readers, and look for other ways to reduce the pressure to buy?

- Could we make it easier for customers to feel they have permission to play, to explore, to hang out?

- Could we listen better to feedback we hear about what people do (and don't) like about shopping at the mall?

No, not all of these ideas are necessarily going to be right for our store…but if we identify just a couple that are, we can transform the experience and make it something people want to repeat.

THREE KEY POINTS ABOUT THIS PROCESS

It was no accident I chose Steve Jobs as the model of behavior in implementing this process. He was a master at it. He created user experiences like no one else, and as a result, he built a company like no other. His best practices are worth studying closely. In particular, I'd like to call your attention to three critical best practices Jobs left behind as legacies for all of us who follow him and aspire to contribute and innovate at the level he did. I make a point of reminding my clients to model all three of these best practices as they design their own Uncopyable experience. They are briefly summarized below.

1. **Think *before* and *after* the touchpoints you are used to considering.** Jobs and his team were not just designing touchpoints that resided within the store; they were designing touchpoints for people approaching it (that impossible-to-miss glass storefront and the door built into it), as well as touchpoints for the moment *after* someone walked out the door (once you make a purchase at the store, you carry it out in an Apple-branded shopping bag, which of course turns you into a walking billboard for Apple!). The

user experience may begin long before you imagine, and it may continue for long after you imagine. Design as much of it as you can.

2. **Consider both the visible and the invisible journey.** The touchpoints visible to the end user are only half the story. Things that are never seen by the end user can have an immense impact on his or her experience. A whole series of *invisible* touchpoints that make that experience possible have to be consciously designed as well. For instance: What, specifically, should the person welcoming people into the Apple Store say as an initial greeting? Who is the ideal candidate for this job? How much improvising should that person do? What must the person always say? What must the person *never* say? How, specifically, should the greeter handle the different levels of familiarity with Apple products that visitors present with? How should the greeter explain the Genius Bar process for someone who has never used the Genius Bar? All of these questions must be considered and answered ahead of time. *Every* touchpoint that has an external impact carries with it a series of internal touchpoints that require careful design.

Another example is to think of this from a B2B perspective. What are those jobs, operations, or other types of tasks that are invisible to the customer yet still impact their overall experience? Accounting? Delivery? Repair? Inventory? We might not normally think of those areas in planning the customer's experience, but if they don't operate seamlessly, the customer WILL be affected!

3. **Don't just listen to what the end user tells you...anticipate what the end user *would* tell you they wanted if they knew what was possible.** It's highly likely Jobs heard *direct* feedback from any number of sources that they often felt pressured to buy by tech salespeople when they visited retail computer outlets. But it's hard to envision shoppers asking him for a store without cash registers, because most consumers were not (and are not) used to thinking that way. Be ready to take what you hear from the end user and extend it to the next level of convenience, seamlessness, and ease of use. If Jobs had not excelled at this, he would never have launched the iPhone!

> **"Some people say, 'Give the customers what they want.' But that's not my approach. Our job is to figure out what they're going to want before they do. I think Henry Ford once said, 'If I'd asked customers what they wanted, they would have told me, "A faster horse!"'"**
>
> **—Steve Jobs**

So now, let's say we're conducting this process of *Choreographing the Uncopyable Experience* for a hospital. In alignment with the first best practice mentioned above, we're going to ask ourselves, *What are the pre- and post-treatment touchpoints that impact the patient experience?* We're going to talk to patients and their families about this, and if we find out the treatment and care experience is superb, but the getting-out-of-the-parking-lot experience is a nightmare, we're going to redesign the parking lot experience!

In alignment with the second best practice, we're going to make sure we design, test, and troubleshoot all the *internal* processes that support each *external* touchpoint a patient or a patient's family experiences. We're not going to assume people know how to (for instance) navigate the parking lot and exit the hospital. If they need someone who can help them make sense of the system, we're going to create a clear set of support instructions for internal staff, and we're going to train and deploy people who are tasked with making sure the exit from the parking lot is a positive experience.

In alignment with the third best practice, we're going to find a way to leave a positive impression on the patient and the patient's family that no one else is leaving, one that patients haven't even thought about yet. We might use the principle of inversion to create a parallel position to the greeter—someone whose job it is to ensure patients make it all the way out of the hospital parking lot without experiencing any confusion, technical disorientation, or stress!

THE BIG TAKEAWAY:

Choreograph a user experience others cannot or will not offer.

DO THIS:

Chart the experience your clients or customers currently have.

Assess all the touchpoints—the before and after touchpoints, ones both visible and invisible to the end user—and determine how you can choreograph a seamless, memorable, Uncopyable customer experience. Ask yourself:

- Which touchpoints do we have control over?
- Which touchpoints are we basically copying from our competition?
- Can we redesign any of those touchpoints as our own?
- How many touchpoints can we redesign or create to construct an experience that allows us to stand out from the competition?

Be sure to consider both the visible and invisible touchpoints.

GET THE "STEALING GENIUS FIELD GUIDE" PLUS MORE USEFUL INFORMATION AND TIPS! GO TO:

stealinggenius.com/resources

Ideas for Stealing Genius

CH 8

STEALING GENIUS LEVEL 7: BRING IN A STEALING GENIUS SENSEI

"We don't see the world as it is, we see it as we are." —Anaïs Nin

The seventh Stealing Genius level is *Bring in a Stealing Genius Sensei*. If you've familiarized yourself with Levels 1 through 6 and you're still looking for more guidance and support, this level is where you may want to go.

I referred to George de Mestral and Isaac Newton as Stealing Genius Black Belts. They both had developed 24/7 awareness of the world around them. They achieved Stealing Genius Level 5 on their own, and both changed the world.

The term "black belt" is commonly connected to martial arts. I studied Chinese martial arts for a number of years, climbing from the beginner's white belt to orange, then blue, green, and brown. The final level is black.[1] It took me a few years to get to brown, but it would have taken several more to achieve black. It's really difficult. I didn't make it.

The thing is, even black belts have teachers. At my school, we called him "shifu." A more commonly known title is "sensei." If you want to achieve black belt, you need a sensei. In the context of Stealing Genius, a sensei is someone from the outside who serves as the "alien"—the ultimate outsider—and leads a comprehensive, ongoing discussion about innovation at your organization.

Many entrepreneurs, company founders, and other senior executives who are used to "going it alone" are not particularly curious about this level of the Stealing Genius process when they first encounter it. There are a lot of variations on the way this resistance can be expressed, but the most common pushback sounds something like this:

Our product/service/platform is so cutting-edge, so powerful, so well designed and executed that it will create (or has already created) a powerful competitive advantage for us. We don't need to bring someone in. We don't need to invest in innovation for next quarter, next season, next year. What we need to do is capitalize on what we have already developed. That's our priority—delivering value to the customer with what we have right now.

Whether or not you opt to begin working with a Stealing Genius Sensei, let me suggest you take a close look at how that resistance translates in terms of working assumptions for the business. What these leaders are really saying is this:

Innovation is not a priority right now, because what we have is so mind-blowing that everyone will want it indefinitely.

It is entirely understandable that entrepreneurs and other leaders would buy into this idea. After all, they are heavily invested in their company, its mission, and the value they deliver to end users. It is only natural for them to think of their latest product, their latest service, their latest big idea, their latest breakthrough as the ultimate game-changer.

In the beginning, maybe it was. But as time and technology move forward, we inevitably find that the game-changer has been copied and possibly bettered. Let me be 100 percent blunt. Technology is commoditizing everything. That's reality. Do we recognize that reality? If we don't, we may fall into the trap of protecting the status quo. Do we really want our long-term strategic focus to be "Protect the cash cow"? Eventually, as we all know, the cash cow dies.

I get it, though. It's natural for leaders to persuade themselves the cash cow *won't* die. But that way of thinking is simply not accurate. Not only that—it's dangerous to the future of any company. Cash cows die all the time.

Let me be 100 percent blunt. Technology is commoditizing everything. Cash cows die all the time.

MILLER'S LAW

One of the most important jobs the Stealing Genius Sensei has—and one of this book's most important objectives—is to disabuse senior leadership of the notion that what they have to offer right now is so amazing they can put innovation on the back burner for a while.

Innovation can *never* be put on the back burner. It must *always* be one of the critical, top-tier priorities for your organization if your company is to become competitive, remain competitive, and thrive over the long term. That's because of something I call Miller's Law.

Miller's Law reads as follows:

If something is successful and copyable, it will be copied.

What this means in practice is that there is *no* one product, *no* one service, *no* one application you can count on to distinguish yourself from the competition and secure loyalty from customers over the long term.

Innovation can *never* be put on the back burner.

TECHNOLOGY COMMODITIZES EVERYTHING

Technology will turn even your hottest product, your coolest cutting-edge application, your best service strategy into a commodity. Why? Because today's barrier-busting design, production, and communication platforms *guarantee* you will eventually be copied and subjected to price pressures from others who deliver essentially the same thing. And as we have seen earlier in this book, once you start playing the who-has-the-lowest-price game, *you lose. You do not want to get into a race to the bottom!*

It's extremely difficult today, and in most cases impossible, to create a sustainable, Uncopyable competitive advantage with a new product, a new service, a new application. No matter what you come up with, you have to assume someone else is going to notice it, reverse engineer it, and imitate it with increasing skill and decreasing margin, until they're basically offering exactly or slightly better than what you're offering. For less money. In more and more cases, you won't have months or years until this happens. You'll have weeks.

And something else important needs to be pointed out here, something that takes us well beyond products, services, and applications. Remember what Deming told me about total quality, which I shared with you back at the beginning of the book: the operative word is never *quality*. The operative word there is *total*. When you develop a total-quality philosophy, it's a wall-to-wall and floor-to-ceiling proposition. It affects everything! So the clients I work with have used the concepts I'm sharing with you in this book to raise their game in *every* realm of the business, not just in the product and service offerings the customer sees. They're Stealing Genius in order to improve their marketing, their branding, their operations, their production, their warehousing, their accounting—you name it. They are out to improve everything, in short, that has *any impact*, visible or invisible, on the customer's experience with the company.

This is the key point. We are not *just* looking at how to make the product, service, or application better. We are looking at how to design, live, and support a culture of *constant innovation* that connects to anything and everything in the business that can impact the customer. Which is everything! Remember what Peter Drucker said: "Because its purpose is to create a customer, the business enterprise has two—and only these two—basic functions: *marketing* and *innovation*."

So now we face a critical challenge. A great product, service, or application does not create an Uncopyable competitive advantage for very long. And you know what else? The "best" customer service does not create that Uncopyable competitive advantage for very long, either…because what constitutes "great service" varies so dramatically from person to person.

So what *does*?

Here's the answer: a new *experience.*

And that is what the Stealing Genius Sensei is there to help you define, create, execute, deliver consistently, and support: a new *high-value-added experience*, one that builds a powerful emotional attachment with a clearly defined group of customers—your moose.

PART OF THE CLUB

You want the people you are targeting to see themselves as part of an elite club. And the most powerful way to do that is to give them a new experience they can get only by interacting with you! So these are the essential questions the sensei is going to bring you back to again and again and again: *What is the experience we are creating? How does it create extraordinary value? And how does it create an emotional, Uncopyable attachment?*

That's a much bigger priority than the questions most companies focus on, which typically sound like this: *What new products, what new services, what new applications can we offer?*

One of the big reasons leaders can often benefit from working with a Stealing Genius Sensei is that they have been asking themselves those kinds of limiting questions for years. They have fallen, over and over again, into the trap of aiming to design a better product, or aiming to improve customer service, or aiming to create a new application, and inevitably they do that from within their own box, observing and copying their competition, without even realizing they've boxed themselves in.

Sometimes it takes an "alien" to change the frame of reference and get us out of that box, so we can design an experience that delivers a level of emotional impact that gets people to want to come back to our club—and bring others with them. Here is the point: by working directly with such an "alien" in real time, you can dramatically speed up the process by which you create the kinds of experiences that draw people into your club, keep them coming back, and turn them into evangelists for your brand.

The Stealing Genius Sensei is there to remind you, constantly and from multiple directions, that what people are actually buying is the *experience* that makes them feel like they belong to a club. The product or service that connects to that feeling is just the means to an end. The experience must come first, and it must be refined and improved constantly.

The reason to work with such a sensei is simple: It takes time and practice to learn to think this way. It takes time and practice to step away from what we're used to. It takes time and practice to learn to *follow the experience* in a way that supports a culture of innovation.

Let me share with you a particularly powerful example of what I am talking about, a true story illustrating exactly how a Stealing Genius master thinks.

FOLLOW THE EXPERIENCE

One weekend day in the early 1950s, Walt Disney took his kids out to visit a merry-go-round. (If anyone from history is a Stealing Genius Black Belt, it's Walt Disney!)

Disney was deeply disappointed at the condition of the ride his daughters took, and he was unimpressed by the attitude of the employees operating it. The carousel looked run-down, the paint and varnish were chipped and faded, many of the horses that were supposed to go up and down didn't work. Not only that—the attendants looked like they would rather have been anywhere else than interacting with kids.

This was supposed to be Disney's day out with his two daughters, but the experience he and his kids had encountered left a lot to be desired. So he did what great innovators always do: he followed the experience he wanted to create. He started asking big questions: *What would a better experience for families look like, sound like, and feel like?*

"I felt that there should be some kind of an amusement enterprise built, where parents and their children could have fun together," Disney would recall years later. Notice that Disney, a movie studio head, was focusing, not on what kind of movie his studio could make next, not on the technical features of the next world-class merry-go-round, and not on what other amusement parks were doing or had done.

He was focusing on the *experience* parents and children could have together.

Disney built his own box. He set his team to work on a new project, an entirely different kind of experience, one that would create a whole new playing field by delivering a powerful, positive new emotional experience for families.

That project eventually became known as Disneyland.

BUILD YOUR OWN BOX

Since we are on the topic of amusement parks, I have a question to ask you, a question I often ask audiences and clients: What is the most-ridden roller-coaster in the world?

People come up with all kinds of initial answers to this question. Most of those answers give me clear evidence of the kind of box they have built for themselves around the idea of "roller-coaster." They'll say things like "Kingda Ka at Six Flags" or "the Millennium Force out at Cedar Point." In other words, they hear the word "roller-coaster" and their mind goes and finds the box in their mental inventory labeled "roller-coaster" and then examines the contents of that box based on what is most familiar to them about roller-coasters.

Occasionally, someone gets it and figures out my trick question. Usually, though, hardly ever does anyone move beyond the paradigm. Hardly ever does anyone build their own box. Hardly ever does anyone stop to ask themselves whether the most-ridden roller-coaster might be the one that offers the most memorable and powerful *emotional experience*—and that it might not even be something that looks like a roller-coaster from a distance!

As it happens, the most-ridden roller-coaster in the world is Space Mountain at Disney World. The *reason* it's the most-ridden roller-coaster in the world is not that it's the highest, or the fastest, or the scariest roller-coaster. It's not any of those things. It does not *look* anything like a roller-coaster from the outside. But it *is* the roller-coaster that creates the most compelling and memorable emotional experience for people!

If you didn't think of Space Mountain right away (and it's okay if you didn't)…if you started rummaging around all the boxes you had previously put in your mental warehouse that had the label "roller-coaster" pasted on the outside (and again, it's fine if you did that)…it's very likely you were operating from within a box that was already quite familiar to you.

Innovation dies when we keep going to the same box over and over again. Why not build a new box, one nobody has ever used before? Working with a Stealing Genius Sensei can help to expand the number of boxes you draw inspiration from—and then use that expansion, that tidal wave of new influences, new inspirations, new role models, new perspectives to create a brand-new box, one that is utterly your own.

CAN YOU REALLY SEE THINGS "THROUGH THE CUSTOMER'S EYES"?

A critical requirement of creating the kind of experience customers decide to return to again and again is taking the customer's expectations, desires, and driving motivations into account. That sounds simple enough, and yet it often proves extremely difficult in practice. We are told over and over again to "look at it through the customer's eyes" and to "take the customer's side" in our discussions…but is that even possible?

The simple answer is one that surprises a lot of people: not really. In most cases, it's *not* possible to see things through the eyes of your customer. The possible exception to this is when we really *are* a customer. If we decide to buy something from our own company's website to see what happens, or to pick up the phone and call the helpline to get a product question resolved, then there's a (limited) opportunity to directly experience what the customer experiences. But even then we don't have precisely the same insights, motivations, and reactions that a customer will, and so our picture is, by definition, going to be incomplete. The reality is, we're *not* the customer, and it's a mistake to pretend we can see things from their perspective. We can see things only from *our* perspective. And that's one of the big reasons some companies decide to work with a Stealing Genius facilitator: to move beyond their own heuristics.

That word *heuristics* may be new to you and potentially even a little intimidating. Here is all you really need to know about heuristics:

Individuals assess probabilities based on their familiarity with a certain task, idea, or environment. Humans attempt to frame a decision based on prior situations confronted and successfully negotiated. Individuals start at one place in a decision matrix and adjust from that initial point.

So when we talk about heuristics, what are we talking about? We are talking about our own personal history, our own experiences, our own predispositions, our own habitual thought patterns, our own ways of making decisions when we are exposed to new information, new circumstances, new issues, and new people. Our heuristics are not right or wrong. They're just incomplete, because we can't possibly take all the other relevant perspectives, experiences, and issues into account—even if we imagine we can. *This is why it is often so difficult for us to move beyond our own assumptions and preconceptions.* Our heuristics are forever pointing us toward our own perspective and our own experiences.

Heuristics are who you are. They are the assumptions and decision-making processes that have been embedded in your life from both nature and nurture. They are how your family taught you to think and how the School of Life taught you to think. They're what you believe in. They're your perspective on the world. They're all the experiences you had growing up with your family, with your friends, with your church, with your school, with the sports that you play—whatever it was you did that impacted how you see the world right now. Heuristics simply means you see the world through your eyes.

So: When we talk about our heuristics, we are talking, inevitably, about our own perspective and our own bias.

Of course, we can't always know what our bias is or how it is likely to express itself. We can't know what we are leaving out of the picture, what we are adding to the picture, or even if we're Photoshopping the picture. We just know we are creating a picture. Sometimes we label that picture "reality." And that is the tricky part about any discussion of heuristics. It is in the very nature of bias that the person who has a bias at first considers it to be "the way things really are." But if we want to make good decisions, we need to understand that as tempting as it may be to believe that our assessment of a situation is "the way things really are," we're simply wrong.

Heuristics have been described as "mental shortcuts that ease the cognitive load of making a decision."[2] One classic example of such a shortcut is attribute substitution, which is something that happens without our conscious awareness. For instance: When presented with a complex set of options as we consider products on a shelf, we may end up selecting, not the option that connects most directly to the solution to our problem, but the option that seems most *familiar* to us. The operative word there is "seems." Something as inconsequential as the color of a label or the shape of a bottle can trigger the feeling of familiarity that justifies a purchase decision. Perhaps we used something shaped like that bottle, with that colored label, in the past when we faced a similar situation. Perhaps we don't even realize that's what is influencing our decision. But it is.

TWO UNIQUE EXPERIENCES

I grew up in a small town in southern Indiana, back in the 1960s: Columbus, Indiana. Columbus was not very big. Still isn't. There was one high school in the town at that time; it was a big high school. It served kids from the whole of Bartholomew County. So we had about 3,000 kids attending classes. Our basketball arena seated over 7,000. At the time, as far as I could tell, pretty much everybody was white. We had a handful of black students in our class. One of the black students—I'll call him Matt—was someone with whom I had hardly any interaction at all as a teenager. Years later, I got to know Matt as an adult through reunions, and we've shared a lot of stories about Columbus, Indiana.

It's really, really hard to see things through the customer's eyes.

Why do I share this information with you? Because if you were to ask me what it was like to grow up in Columbus, I would give you an answer based on *my* heuristics. And if you were to ask Matt the same question, he would give you an answer based on *his* heuristics. And you might conclude that we were talking about two entirely different towns! Why? Because I was looking at Columbus through my eyes, and Matt was looking at it through his. I never had the experience (for instance) of being taken to a restaurant, only to have the waiter announce the chef had taken ill and it wasn't possible to serve my party and perhaps we could come back another night. I never had the experience of going to a bar as a young man of legal drinking age and being told to enter by the back door. Matt *did* have those kinds of experiences, over and over again. And many worse. So any summary I can give you about what it was like to grow up and live in Columbus is, by definition, going to be limited and incomplete. I was seeing life in Columbus through my eyes. Matt was seeing it through his eyes. We had starkly different assumptions and experiences about "the way things really were" in that town.

Here is the point: it's really, really hard to see things through the customer's eyes. We each have our own history, our own perspective, our own way of learning things, evaluating things, understanding things, solving things. That's nothing to apologize for. It's part of being human. But if we are serious about understanding someone else—our target customer, also known as our "moose," for instance—then we will probably want to work with someone who specializes in helping us move *beyond* our own familiar frame of reference. We will want to work with someone who will help us tackle questions that simply would not occur to us, someone who is looking at the world in a very different way than we are used to looking at it. Because our way of considering our situation is likely to be leaving out important pieces of the picture! That's a big part of what a Stealing Genius facilitator can bring to an organization: the ability to isolate the target customer's heuristics—which may, for any number of reasons, be very different from our own.

We should not expect another person's heuristics to match up with ours.

THE BIG TAKEAWAY:

A Stealing Genius Sensei can help you create, define, execute, deliver consistently, and support a new high-value-added experience, one that builds a powerful emotional attachment.

DO THIS:

Bring in a Stealing Genius facilitator to help you move beyond your familiar frame of reference and create a new, Uncopyable customer experience.

Make innovation a strategic priority.

GET THE "STEALING GENIUS FIELD GUIDE" PLUS MORE USEFUL INFORMATION AND TIPS! GO TO:

stealinggenius.com/resources

NOTES

1. I know. I know. Some martial arts have many more colors and even different degrees of a color, including black. The highest level I've ever heard of is tenth-level black belt. I would want anybody with that designation to be my friend.

2. "Heuristic," *Wikipedia*, last updated August 7, 2021, https://en.wikipedia.org/wiki/Heuristic.

Ideas for Stealing Genius

STAY IN TOUCH!

In order to be successful both today and in the future, we can use the breakthrough principle of Stealing Genius to separate ourselves from the competition. We can do that by delivering an experience, and a level of emotional connection, the competition either cannot or will not attempt to copy…or that the competition will, as a practical matter, be *unable* to copy.

In this book, I've shared seven powerful tools for doing just that. I hope you will keep in touch with me and let me know about how these ideas have worked for you. You can always contact me at theadventure.com. Until then, remember:

Don't Just Get Out Of The Box…
STEAL GENIUS
AND
BUILD YOUR OWN BOX!

ABOUT THE AUTHOR

Steve Miller is the author of the bestseller, ***UNCOPYABLE: How to Create an Unfair Advantage Over Your Competition***. For 35 years, he has taught small- to medium-size B2B organizations, teams, and marketers how to use marketing and branding effectively and profitably. He has facilitated hundreds of organizations in 129 different industries to separate themselves meaningfully from the competition, leveraging innovative strategies and tools to facilitate rapid growth, even during COVID.

Known for his edgy, rebellious, no-spin-zone perspective, Steve is the son of the coinventor of the 8-track; he non-profitably played on the PGA Tour, double-jacked 1,500 feet down in the copper mines of Arizona, and even worked in front of the camera in Hollywood (all of which means he's 100% unemployable).

Steve has delivered over *1,600 presentations* around the world, including at the prestigious main TED Conference. Besides his eight books, Steve has written for and been featured in over 250 publications, including *Fast Company*, *Businessweek*, *Fortune*, *The Wall Street Journal*, *The Washington Post*, *SUCCESS*, *Association Management*, and *Highlights for Children*. (Okay, he made that last one up.)

His smokin' hot wife, Kay, and world's funniest and most beautiful daughter, Kelly, are his #1 priority.

More about Steve, including his contact information, can be found at www.stealinggenius.com.

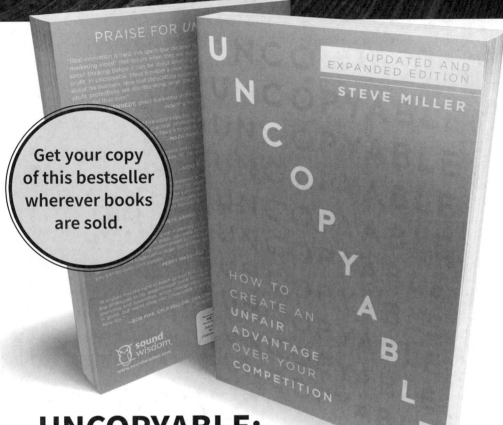

Connect with Steve!

 theadventure.com/

 facebook.com/theadventurellc/

 twitter.com/steveamiller

 youtube.com/steveamiller/

 linkedin.com/in/steveamiller/

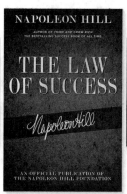